Amplify Your Ministry

With Miracles & Manifestations of the Holy Spirit

DAG HEWARD-MILLS

Parchment House

Unless otherwise stated, all Scripture quotations are taken from the
King James Version of the Bible

AMPLIFY YOUR MINISTRY
WITH MIRACLES AND MAnifestations of The Holy Spirit

Excerpts from: Welcoming a Visitation of the Holy Spirit, by Wesley
Campbell, Published by Strang Communications.
The Power of Faith, Article in October 1999 issue of Reader's Digest,
author Phyllis McIntosh. All excerpts used by permission.

[77]Find out more about Dag Heward-Mills at:
Healing Jesus Campaign
Write to: evangelist@daghewardmills.org
Website: www.daghewardmills.org
Facebook: Dag Heward-Mills
Twitter: @EvangelistDag

ISBN 13: 978-9988-8550-3-1

Contents

CHAPTER 1

Why Miracles and Manifestations of the Spirit Will Amplify Your Ministry

Miracles and manifestations are our only chance to reach the world for Jesus Christ. They are our only chance to reach every kindred, nation and people for the Kingdom. They are the opportunities for ministers to accomplish what God has called them for.

Miracles and manifestations of the Spirit were available to the twelve disciples and for the seventy people that Jesus sent out. They are still available for all of us through the Great Commission. They are for all of us if we will begin to know and realize what God has given to us.

1. Miracles and manifestations of the Spirit will help you reach the world for Christ.

Once, when election results were released from the different regions of my country, I realized how many millions of souls lived in remote regions. God's heart is bleeding for lost souls. There is no need for us to bow to political pressure to provide social services for the nation. It is not the provision of social services like schools and universities that make us useful to the nation.

The church is a special institution anointed by God with special power and anointing. By that power and anointing, we will be able to do what God has called us to do. He has chosen preaching, teaching and healing as His method for helping lost humanity.

2. Miracles and manifestations of the Spirit will cause you to come out of obscurity.

You need to come out of obscurity! Your ministry needs to be felt and seen in the world! What is the use of your great wisdom if it is not heard, and if it is not seen? Jesus was brought up in an insignificant carpenter's home, but God gave Him something special. What would bring Jesus out of obscurity? What would make anyone listen to His message? What could Jesus do without modern methods of advertisement? Miracles and manifestations of the Spirit are what brought Jesus out of obscurity.

Miracles and manifestations of the Spirit are your chance to rise out of obscurity. Jesus never wrote a book, travelled in a car, took a train or plane but he became famous.

The Bible says that, His fame spread abroad, and the whole city gathered at his door (Mark. 1:28,33). If we want the cities of this world to gather at the door of our crusades, then we need the healing anointing.

If we want the cities of this world to gather in our churches, then miracles and manifestations of the spirit are the key. The healing anointing will bring the whole city to your door so that you can tell them about Jesus Christ.

3. Miracles and manifestations of the Spirit will attract many broken-hearted people to your ministry.

Jesus said that He was anointed to heal the broken-hearted. There is more to having a broken heart than breaking up with your boyfriend or girlfriend. Broken hearts are caused by disappointments in general. Many people have been surprised by what life has brought them. People live as though everything is okay but they are bleeding, disappointed and hurting inside.

Many of man's problems cannot be cured by drugs, by the psychologist or by the psychiatrist. Many people need a touch from God to give them hope. God is in the business of coming into people's lives to heal their broken hearts.

Many politicians wonder why people keep coming to church because they think that pastors are just taking money from the masses. They wonder why people do not see through the supposed "deception". You see, the problems that people have are often not apparent. People are smiling on the outside but are crying on the inside. Those who criticize the church don't know what the church does for people.

I remember watching an interview of a famous healing evangelist on television. He was asked many questions about his salary, his houses and his cars. The talk show host was trying to make him look foolish.

Then they opened the phone lines and a gentleman called in to be prayed for. Suddenly the atmosphere changed. The caller had cancer and was dying. He wanted the evangelist to pray for him. All the cynical questions that the host had asked meant nothing now. The television host was faced with a desperate, weepy caller who urgently needed help. Only the evangelist could offer that help. The relevance of the evangelist's ministry was obvious to all. More people kept calling and asking for prayer for their desperate and hopeless conditions.

People have needs and the healing anointing will meet those needs. When you have the power of God with miracles and manifestations of the Spirit, the broken-hearted will flock to you.

4. Miracles and manifestations of the Spirit will make your ministry relevant to the society.

"To be relevant" means "to be important". We become relevant to the world when the healing anointing is in operation. It is when the broken-hearted are restored and the poor have the good news preached to them that we become relevant. Evil spirits torment people and bring fear into their lives. The healing anointing will deliver people from evil spirits.

Many nations are ruled by fear and superstition. Through miracles and manifestations of the Spirit the curses are broken and healing comes. Many people understand supernatural power. If you have the healing anointing, you can stand before natives who dabble in evil supernatural power and challenge them! If you just have a little Sunday school sermon, you will be no match for the witches and wizards of our time.

There is so much superstition in our world. There are rivers where fishing is not allowed! Sometimes people are not even allowed to fetch water from these rivers. There are dams that cannot be built because of superstition. People are afraid of so many different things. Sometimes out of superstition, we fear to put on certain clothes at certain times. You cannot put streetlights on certain roads because of the presence of gods who supposedly inhabit these roads. People are afraid to use certain roads at certain times. They are afraid to turn off the lights. People are sometimes afraid to travel on Fridays. There is a kind of superstition surrounding travelling on the 13th of any particular month. If the 13th falls on a Friday, it makes it worse. Even airlines are aware of this. There is no seat number thirteen in many aircrafts. There is no thirteenth floor in many apartment buildings.

One day, I was travelling on an aircraft. We had a rough landing and the pilot apologized for that and explained that the reason for the rough landing was because it was Friday, the 13th.

Mercy! Many people live in fear.

The church becomes relevant when it has something to offer. We become relevant when we have the answers to people's needs. No government can offer what the church offers through the power of the Holy Spirit. No politician can give what the church gives. Neither teachers nor medical doctors can give what the church gives. Only God can heal the broken hearts and save the people. Every part of the world needs the miracles and manifestations of the Holy Spirit.

Our relevance as a church does not come about by starting schools or universities. The government is the one supposed to provide education. When the church does provide education, it must be seen as what it really is – a love gift to that nation. The salvation of mankind is provided through the cross of Jesus Christ.

We have been charged with the Great Commission. No other institution has been charged with this Great Commission. Our relevance comes from preaching and teaching about Jesus. Our relevance comes from healing the sick. Our relevance comes through the miracles and the manifestation of the power of the Holy Spirit.

5. Miracles and manifestations of the Spirit will draw captive souls to your church.

Many people are possessed with devils. One day, I saw a friend of mine who was high on drugs. I just felt so sad. Only the power of God can deliver people from drugs, alcohol, and immorality. Many people are bound. They cannot set themselves free. The healing anointing will set people free from everything that keeps them in bondage.

Miracles and manifestations of the Spirit will give hope to barren women. I happened to watch a documentary in which a snake was inserted into a woman as a treatment for infertility. She had been to see a fetish priest for help and this is the kind of help they had given her to enable her have a child.

I said to myself, "The difficulties of infertility are beyond comprehension." We are all so afraid of snakes that we do not even want to go near them when they are caged. We have goose pimples when we even see a snake on television. To see a woman willingly permit a snake to be inserted into her body in order to have a baby shows the extent of her need.

People have asked me why I left the medical profession to preach. They wonder if I am doing anything important as a preacher. What I do today is far more important than practising medicine. If Jesus could have helped the world better through medicine, He would have been a doctor. But he was a preacher and that should tell you something!

Jesus announced that He had come to set at liberty them that were bruised. A bruised person is someone who is hurt. Life is full of pain, hurt and disappointments, and Jesus' healing anointing is to heal the hurt and the bruised.

The Spirit of the Lord is upon me, because he hath anointed me to preach the gospel to the poor; he hath sent me to heal the brokenhearted, to preach deliverance to the captives and recovering of sight to the blind, to set at liberty them that are bruised,

Luke 4:18

Elisha went to heal the waters of a town because there was something wrong with the water.

"And the men of the city said unto Elisha, Behold, I pray thee, the situation of this city is pleasant, as my lord seeth: but the water is naught, and the ground barren. And he said, Bring me a new cruse, and put salt therein. And they brought it to him. And he went forth unto the spring of the waters, and cast the salt in there, and said, Thus saith the LORD, I have healed these waters; there shall not be from thence any more death or barren land. So the waters were healed unto this day, according to the saying of Elisha which he spake" (2 Kings 2:19-22).

When God heals your waters, He is meeting the basic needs of your life. God is showing you that there are many needy people in this world. There are people who have no treatment for their sicknesses. In poor countries, some women deliver their babies under trees. This is why we are anointed to preach the gospel to the poor.

The poor of this world far outnumber the rich. God is extending our hearts to the poor. You cannot go to the poor of this world and talk to them unless you have some good news. They want to know how the gospel will practically affect their lives. How can they understand the doctrines of the gospel with all their problems, their sicknesses and their extreme poverty?

We need to pray for more miracles. Our hearts must desire more miracles! Otherwise, we will continue to stay in our little corners having a good time while the masses go to Hell.

6. **Miracles and manifestations of the Spirit will magnify God in your ministry.**

Heal me, O LORD, and I shall be healed; save me and I shall be saved: for thou art my praise.
Jeremiah 17:14

Jeremiah cried, "Heal me O Lord and I shall be healed!" If God heals you, you are really healed! If God saves you, you are really saved! The healing methods of man are greatly deficient. Through the healing anointing, you will magnify the role that God can play in people's lives.

The fact that God heals does not mean that He does not approve of medical science. God is not against medicine. In fact, the intelligence that has been given to human beings to develop drugs is from God. He is the source of that gift. As a doctor, I believe in medical science. Thank God for medical science and for doctors. We cannot do without them.

However, God has more in store for us than medical science. He can do what medical science cannot do. He does things which medical science cannot do. Sometimes, he does things that medical science can do. All we know is that he does good things.

I like telling the story of a man who was saved from an earthquake in San Francisco. He was interviewed after his earthquake experience. He had survived three days and nights during the earthquake, under the building and in the rubble. He was asked how he had been able to stay alive under the collapsed building for such a long time.

He answered, "I am a man of strong will power. When I determine to do something, nothing can stop me. I am able to stay on course! I don't swerve to the left or to the right! I am a man of strong determination and will power and so I refused to die! I was determined to live and that is why I believe I stayed alive!"

His wife was interviewed as well. She said, "Well, I know my husband and I have been married to him for many years. He is a man of very strong will power! When he determines to do something, nothing can move him to the left or to the right. He is a firm man. He is a very determined person. He carries through his projects! He moves forward. He is the type who does not waver in spite of adversities. I know my man! I've been married to him for twenty-seven years so when he determined he would live, he just stayed alive."

This man's doctor was interviewed as well. He was asked, "What do you have to say about your patient who has survived this amazing experience?" He answered, "Well, I know my patient; he is a man of very strong will power. He has survived because will power is very important in a patient's life. When a patient decides to die, he dies. When he decides to live, he lives."

Can you believe that eight days later, this man with the strong will power was struck with a heart attack? He died instantly! Then I asked myself, "Where was his will power?"

The tractors and bulldozers seemed to have saved him. The doctors seemed to have resuscitated him. But he was not really saved. He was actually just about to die!

That is why we must turn our eyes to the Lord and say, "Heal me, oh Lord and I will be healed. Save me and I will be saved." It is when the Lord stretches out His hand to heal you that you will be truly healed.

7. **Miracles and manifestations of the Spirit will greatly promote the Kingdom of God.**

And heal the sick that are therein, and say unto them, The kingdom of God is come nigh unto you.
                                                            Luke 10:9

The arrival of the Kingdom of God is demonstrated by the undoing of the things that were done by the devil's kingdom.

That is why Jesus healed the sick. He undid the sicknesses that were brought on by the devil. He cast out evil spirits, which had inhabited human beings.

The devil has distorted nature; that is why storms and earthquakes kill people. Jesus demonstrated His ability to stop all these distortions of nature. That is why He rebuked storms, and walked on the water to demonstrate His power over all the distortions of nature.

Jesus overcame death in order to undo the works of the devil. He raised people from the dead who had been killed by the devil. He demonstrated that the Kingdom of God and the Kingdom of Heaven had actually come. That is why Jesus sent His disciples to go and heal the sick and inform them that the Kingdom of God had arrived. The sign of the new kingdom was the undoing of the works of the devil.

And the seventy returned again with joy, saying, Lord, even the devils are subject unto us through thy name.
                                                            Luke 10:17

8. **Miracles and manifestations of the Spirit will release joy in your ministry.**

And the seventy returned again with joy, saying, Lord, even the devils are subject unto us through thy name.
                                                            Luke 10:17

There is much joy when you see the power of God manifested. You begin to get excited. Some people do not know that the Kingdom of God is exciting. The only excitement they have is in nightclubs and in worldly pleasures. When you do the work of God in His way, you experience such joy and excitement beyond description. That is why the Bible says the seventy returned with joy. Demons ran and fled as they prayed. Sicknesses were healed. The healing anointing is our chance for a certain level of joy and excitement. I believe that God is bringing that rejoicing back into our midst.

9. Miracles and manifestations of the Spirit will enhance your pastoral ministry.

I am the good shepherd: ...

John 10:11

Jesus was the good shepherd and the best example of a pastor. He operated with miracles and mighty manifestations of the Holy Spirit. What about you? Are you a good pastor? You must be like Jesus if you want to be a good pastor and operate in mighty manifestations of the Spirit.

It is difficult to gather one hundred people in a room or under a tree. People have interesting programmes to watch on television. There are lots of things to entertain the people of today. People will not just leave their pleasures to attend your boring church service. Miracles and manifestations of the Spirit are the chance for pastors to gather crowds for the glory of God.

10. Miracles and manifestations of the Spirit will enhance your teaching ministry.

Miracles and manifestations of the Spirit will make people take your teaching ministry more seriously. When I came into contact with Kenneth Hagin through his books and tapes, I took what he said very seriously because of the supernatural element of his teaching. I noticed that he always shared a lot of supernatural stories when he taught the Word of God. He wrote about his visions and the miracle healings at his meetings. These made me develop a special interest in his other teachings.

If God has called you to be a teacher, the healing anointing is the chance for your teaching ministry to go further than you have ever imagined.

11. Miracles and manifestations of the Spirit will cause you to see the glory of God in every aspect of ministry.

Jesus saith unto her, Said I not unto thee, that, if thou wouldest believe, thou shouldest see the glory of God?

John 11:40

Thank God for preaching and teaching but the healing anointing is our chance for the glory of God. It is our opportunity to see the glory of God. Jesus said, "Did I not tell you, that if you will believe you shall see the glory of God?"

We have to believe in Him. We have to encourage manifestations of the Spirit. We have to say, "Yes, Lord." Preaching and teaching are all part of the power of God. But I am talking about miracles now. The healing anointing is our chance to experience the glory of God.

12. Miracles and manifestations of the Spirit will cause you to go deeper in ministry.

Deep calleth unto deep at the noise of thy waterspouts: all thy waves and thy billows are gone over me.

Psalms 42:7

Miracles and manifestations of the Spirit are your opportunity to go deeper in God. There are deeper things in God! "Deep calls unto deep!" In other words, if you are not deep you cannot reach for the deep things that are in God. Everybody has his deep things. If your "deep" is not calling or speaking, my "deep" will not respond.

When you relate deeply with a person, the "deep" part in you comes forth. But if the conversation we have is "Hi" and "Bye" and "Hello", then the deep part of me will not come forth to you. If you relate shallow things like greetings and questions about the weather, you will receive equally shallow responses. There are obviously deeper things than asking about the family, the weather and the dates for a funeral. When you tell a friend what is in your heart, the deep part in him responds. That is why the Bible says, "deep calls unto deep".

People who are just relating to God on a shallow level are not going to experience the deep things of God. God longs for the deeper part of you to call out to Him. There is more to God than we know. There is more to God than we see. There is more to the ministry than what we are doing. There is more than just preaching and teaching.

God is bringing that "more" into your life. Sometime ago, whilst having a deep relationship with the Lord, the Lord told me that He had given me a healing anointing. He told me He was going to use me in the healing ministry because He had anointed me to heal the sick.

That is why I pray for the sick and preach about miracles. God wants to take you deeper! He wants you to move into miracles and manifestations of the Spirit.

CHAPTER 2

How You Can Amplify Your Ministry through Miracles and Manifestations

Y ou need to fortify your mind with a set of convictions which will stabilize you on your journey into miracle power. It is very easy to stay away from the miracle side of the ministry. It is also easy to start and to stop operating in the ministry of miracles and manifestations of the Spirit. Look around you and you will see that there are few ministers who continue to persist in this type of ministry.

Many ministers are teachers and preachers of good things. Few ministers venture out into the realm of the miraculous and the supernatural. Without a fortified mind and a powerful set of convictions about the power of God and its relevance, you will not get far with this kind of ministry.

This chapter offers you a series of convictions which will help you to enter and to stay in the ministry of miracles and manifestations of the Holy Spirit. Each of these convictions will help you to amplify your ministry through miracles and manifestations of the Holy Spirit.

1. **You will amplify your ministry by believing that your ministry is only validated by miracles and manifestations of the Holy Spirit.**

Ye men of Israel, hear these words; Jesus of Nazareth, a man approved of God among you by miracles and wonders and signs, which God did by him in the midst of you, as ye yourselves also know:

Acts 2:22

Without thinking in a certain way you will never go forward into the miracle ministry. You must believe that miracles, signs and wonders are God's sign of approval on your ministry! How did God approve of Jesus Christ? Through miracles, signs and wonders! How was Jesus' ministry validated? How did John the Baptist know that Jesus Christ was really the Messiah? John the Baptist recognized Jesus Christ because of the miracles He did. When John the Baptist sent a message to Jesus asking if He was the Messiah, Jesus sent back a message saying that the blind were seeing, the deaf were hearing and the dumb were speaking. He said that lepers were being cleansed, and the dead were being raised.

He knew that John the Baptist would understand that the healings were the sign of Christ. He knew that when that message was delivered to John the Baptist, he would know that a new era had begun.

The Old Testament ministers predicted the healing anointing on Jesus but none of them actually ministered healing. Miracles, signs and wonders are a true validation of a New Testament ministry operating in the anointing of Jesus Christ.

2. You will amplify your ministry by believing that a bible-based minister cannot do without miracles and manifestations.

Once your mind is made up that miracles and manifestations of the Spirit are a scriptural part of ministry, they will be included in your life and ministry.

For instance, take a pair of scissors and cut out all the pages and parts of the Bible that talk about miracles. You will find out that you are left with a completely different Bible. The pages of the Bible are replete with miracles and manifestations of the Spirit. God is a God of miracles and power. You cannot separate the work of God from the power of God.

In this modern age, people have gradually moved away from the "power side of God". People have withdrawn from these things and become sceptical. As people have become more and more educated, they have moved away from the supernatural.

Unfortunately, people who believe in miracles are seen as weird and unbalanced. Some have taught that it is poverty and backwardness that make people believe in supernatural power. Because medical science is so advanced, many have thought that miracles are no longer needed. Most Christians do not call for the pastor to lay hands on them or to anoint them with oil when they are sick. We more naturally go to see a doctor.

God is not against medicine. Neither is he against common sense. God is fully aware of the development of medical science and common sense. But He is the same yesterday, today and forever. That means that He is still a healing Jesus, ready and capable of miraculous power demonstration.

3. **You will amplify your ministry by turning away from those who deny the power of miracles and manifestations.**

   This know also, that in the last days perilous times shall come.

   For men shall be lovers of their own selves, covetous, boasters, proud, blasphemers, disobedient to parents, unthankful, unholy, without natural affection, trucebreakers, false accusers, incontinent, fierce, despisers of those that are good, traitors, heady, highminded, lovers of pleasures more than lovers of God; having a form of godliness,

   BUT DENYING THE POWER THEREOF: from SUCH TURN AWAY.

   2 Timothy 3:1-5

Unfortunately, there are some people and some churches that do not accept, recognize, preach about or mention the power of God. There are many good ministers who would talk about good Christian virtues like love, patience etc. but do not go on to talk about the power of God. The Bible has warned that in the last days there will be some people who will have godliness but without power.

According to this Scripture, people who deny the power of God can be godly. Such people will preach about the love of God and will extol Christian virtues but will be silent about the power of God. They may even be against miracles and the power of God. It is important that you turn away from such people if you are to experience the power of God. It is not easy to perform miracles in the presence of scoffers and mockers. The presence of doubting and questioning people is the strongest neutralizing force that kills miracles and manifestations of the Holy Spirit. Jesus Christ could not do many miracles in the presence of questioning and mocking people. This is why many ministers start out performing miracles but end up without a miracle ministry. The questions, the mocking, the scoffing and the doubting of the people around bring an end to every miracle ministry.

> And when the Sabbath had come, He began to teach in the synagogue; and the many listeners were astonished, saying, "Where did this man get these things, and what is this wisdom given to Him, and such miracles as these performed by His hands?
>
> Is not this the carpenter, the son of Mary, and brother of James, and Joses, and Judas, and Simon? Are not His sisters here with us?" And they took offense at Him.
>
> And Jesus said to them, "A prophet is not without honor except in his home town and among his own relatives and in his own household."
>
> And He COULD DO NO MIRACLE there except that He laid His hands upon a few sick people and healed them.
>
> Mark 6:2-5, (NASB)

4. **You will amplify your ministry by believing that you must follow the example of Jesus Christ in miracles and manifestations.**

The Spirit of the Lord is upon me, because he hath anointed me to preach the gospel to the poor; he hath sent me to heal the brokenhearted, to preach deliverance to the captives, and recovering of sight to the blind, to set at liberty them that are bruised,

Luke 4:18

Jesus Christ has had the largest and longest standing ministry ever. If you follow Jesus Christ, your ministry will be amplified a thousand times more than what it is today. So what exactly did Jesus do? Jesus came to this world to save humanity. He was planning to reach everyone with the good news.

Follow the example of Jesus and you will accomplish your goals. You will fulfil your ministry! Follow the example of Jesus and teach the Word of God. Remember that the Word of God is very important no matter how you minister to people. The Word of God must always be taught and spoken. The Bible says that the crowds came to hear Jesus and to be healed. They did not just come to be healed. They came to *hear Him* and to be healed! "And he came down with them, and stood in the plain, and the company of his disciples, and a great multitude of people out of all Judaea and Jerusalem, and from the sea coast of Tyre and Sidon, which came to hear him, and to be healed of their diseases" (Luke 6:17).

He sent his word, and healed them, and delivered *them* from their destructions.

Psalms 107:20

You must follow Jesus' example of ministry. Jesus' ministry was amplified until it reached the whole world. He always sent the Word first and the healing followed. Jesus Christ preached about deliverance. We need to preach certain things if we are going to have them. That is why you must preach about the power of God during miracle services. The Word of God is a seed. The kind of response you get depends on the kind of seed that is sown. You do not get any response before you preach. If I don't preach about it, we are not going to have it.

5. You will amplify your ministry by deciding to walk in the New Testament anointing.

You must believe in your heart that miracles and manifestations of the Spirit are a peculiar gift for those under the new covenant. The manifestations of the Holy Spirit and the miracle healing anointing are peculiar to the New Testament. It is a special anointing that God has available for His church. The healing anointing is a peculiar anointing made available to His church.

Many people think that both the Old and the New Testaments have many miracles. However, a closer look at the Old Testament will reveal very few healing miracles.

The miracles of the Old Testament had to do with the preservation of the nation of Israel. Of all the prophets, Elisha was one of the few who ever ministered to someone who was sick. Abraham also prayed for Abimelech to receive healing under some special circumstances. The rest of the miracles of the Old Testament were miracles of preservation in time of war. Isaac, Jacob, Moses and Elijah never ministered healing to anyone. Isaiah and Jeremiah came around preaching and teaching. Healing did not occur in their ministries.

Miracles and manifestations of the Spirit are characteristic of the New Testament. Walk in the New Testament anointing and accept that you are living in the New Testament era of miracles, signs and wonders.

6. You will amplify your ministry by believing in the prophecies of miracles and manifestations of power.

But unto you that fear my name shall the Sun of righteousness arise with healing in his wings;
Malachi 4:2

Do you want to walk in the fulfilment of prophecy? Or do you want to live your life trying to disprove the prophetic word of God? I would like to flow with the prophetic will of God. The last prophecy of the Old Testament was a prophecy of coming miracle power. The prophecy of healing was the closing prophecy of the Old Testament. The Old Testament closed with a prediction of healing.

The prophet Malachi saw hundreds of years into the future and predicted that there would arise the Sun of righteousness who would be the light of the world. Jesus said, "I am the light of the world." But how would we know who the real Messiah was? The prophet said He would have healing in his wings! Is it any wonder to you that the main characteristic of Jesus' ministry was healing? The main characteristic of your ministry must be healing.

7. **You will amplify your ministry by refusing help from the devil.**

   The spirit of the Lord is upon me because he has anointed me (or equipped me) to preach the gospel to the poor. He has equipped me to heal, to preach deliverance, to set the captives free, to set at liberty them that are bruised and to proclaim the acceptable year of the Lord.

   Luke 4:19

Many ministries are using worldly and demonic methods to reach the world.

Jesus Christ knew that He had something that would help Him save the whole world. Miracles and manifestations of the Holy Spirit! Even the devil knew this and tried to sidetrack the Lord with an offer. On the mount of temptation, the devil offered Jesus a fast and easy way to achieve His goal. The devil said: "Listen, let's make a deal. I will give everything to you right now. You can have it all now. There is a quicker, shorter and simpler way. You do not have to go through all the struggles with the Pharisees and Sadducees."

But Jesus totally ignored the devil and refused Satan's suggestion. He wanted the help of the Holy Spirit and not the help of the devil. Jesus walked away from the mount of temptation and immediately announced how He was going to reach the world with His wonderful message. He announced that He had been anointed with the Holy Spirit to do miracles, signs and wonders. He said, "The spirit of the Lord is upon me because he has anointed me (or equipped me) to preach the gospel to the poor. He has equipped me to heal, to preach deliverance, to set the captives free, to set at liberty them that are bruised and to proclaim the acceptable year of the Lord!"

CHAPTER 3

What Every Minister Should Know about Supernatural Things

Verily, verily, I say unto you, He that believeth on me, the works that I do shall he do also; and greater works than these shall he do; because I go unto my Father.

John 14:12

Contrary to what some people think, your knowledge of the word of God will make you love the supernatural. The Scripture will awaken your interest in supernatural things. This book is about your journey into the supernatural. This book is to awaken your interest in the sensational, dramatic and supernatural dimension of the Holy Spirit. This book is intended to transform you from being an ordinary teacher into a miracle-working teacher.

As you read this book, you can expect to be transformed from being an ordinary pastor into a miracle-working pastor. Perhaps, you have been preaching and teaching the Word of God for years. In spite of your good teachings, you do need the supernatural and power dimension of the Holy Spirit in your ministry.

I became a born-again Christian in the Scripture Union whilst in secondary school. We learnt many important things from the Scripture Union. We learnt how to have a personal "quiet time". We learnt how to study the Bible! We learnt about the importance of the Word of God! We also learnt about the integrity of the Word of God.

Because of this foundation, I have needed to see things in the Word of God before I accept them. I do not agree with or flow in anything not founded in the Word. I want things to be Bible-based, otherwise, they are not good enough. I am grateful to God for this foundational background because it has actually helped me to enter the supernatural dimension of ministry. Everyone needs to move on and build on the foundation that is laid. The Scripture is a good foundation but we must go on and experience all that God has for us.

Seven Things You Should Know about the Supernatural

1. A solid scriptural foundation helps your belief in the supernatural.

Thank God for the Scriptures! It is these Scriptures that show us the supernatural dimension of Christianity. Cut out the supernatural miracles from the Bible and you are left with a book on philosophy.

You cannot avoid the supernatural if you study the Bible. I am always surprised that there are people who do not believe in miracles and yet are committed Christians. Is it intentional blindness?

The Bible directs us to a God who is His Spirit. The Bible teaches us about angels that cannot be seen in the natural. The New Testament is full of instructions concerning the Holy Spirit. In spite of this, many Christians are left out of the blessings of the supernatural.

2. **Many Christians are unaware when they are having supernatural experiences.**

And Jacob went out from Beersheba, and went toward Haran. And he lighted upon a certain place, and tarried there all night, because the sun was set; and he took of the stones of that place, and put them for his pillows, and lay down in that place to sleep.

And he dreamed, and behold a ladder set up on the earth, and the top of it reached to heaven: and behold the angels of God ascending and descending on it. And, behold, the Lord stood above it, and said, I am the Lord God of Abraham thy father, and the God of Isaac: the land whereon thou liest, to thee will I give it, and to thy seed; And thy seed shall be as the dust of the earth, and thou shalt spread abroad to the west, and to the east, and to the north, and to the south: and in thee and in thy seed shall all the families of the earth be blessed.

And, behold, I am with thee, and will keep thee in all places whither thou goest, and will bring thee again into this land; for I will not leave thee, until I have done that which I have spoken to thee of. And Jacob awaked out of his sleep, and he said, SURELY THE LORD IS IN THIS PLACE; AND I KNEW IT NOT.

Genesis 28:10-16

Jacob came to a place, made himself a pillow and lay down to sleep. He had a supernatural experience during the night. When he awoke in the morning he said, "The Lord was in this place, and I knew it not."

This is the testimony of many believers. The Lord is with them and they don't even know it. Angels stand by our side and we are not even aware of it. The Holy Spirit speaks to us and we don't even know it.

It is my prayer, you will soon say, "The Lord was in this place and I knew it!" You will say, "The Holy Spirit was here and I felt Him."

The Supernatural Call of Samson

One of the best examples of discerning the supernatural with your eyes and ears is in the appearance of an angel to Manoah, father of Samson. Samson's mother was in the field when she met a man. But the man that she met was actually an angel! The meeting with the angel was so ordinary that Manoah did not know that he was dealing with an angel. They kept referring to the angel as a man of God because that is what he seemed to be. While the supernatural experience was going on, they were never sure whether they were talking to a man or an angel. Manoah actually asked for the angel's name and address so they could honour him when his prophecy came to pass. How many things have we seen that are supernatural? How many wonderful visions has God given us that we have relegated to the ranks of the ordinary?

And the angel of the Lord appeared unto the woman, and said unto her, Behold now, thou art barren, and bearest not: but thou shalt conceive, and bear a son. Now therefore beware, I pray thee, and drink not wine nor strong drink, and eat not any unclean thing: For, lo, thou shalt conceive, and bear a son; and no razor shall come on his head: for the child shall be a Nazarite unto God from the womb: and he shall begin to deliver Israel out of the hand of the Philistines.

Then the woman came and told her husband, saying, A MAN OF GOD came unto me, and his countenance was like the countenance of AN ANGEL OF GOD, very terrible: but I asked him not whence he was, neither told he me his name:

But he said unto me, Behold, thou shalt conceive, and bear a son; and now drink no wine nor strong drink, neither eat any unclean thing: for the child shall be a Nazarite to God from the womb to the day of his death.

Then Manoah intreated the Lord, and said, O my Lord, let THE MAN OF GOD which thou didst send come again unto us, and teach us what we shall do unto the child that shall be born.

And God hearkened to the voice of Manoah; and the ANGEL OF GOD came again unto the woman as she sat in the field: but Manoah her husband was not with her.

And the woman made haste, and ran, and shewed her husband, and said unto him, Behold, THE MAN HATH APPEARED unto me, that came unto me the other day.

And Manoah arose, and went after his wife, and CAME TO THE MAN, and said unto him, ART THOU THE MAN that spakest unto the woman? And he said, I am.

Judges 13:3-11

And Manoah said unto the angel of the LORD, I pray thee, let us detain thee, until we shall have made ready a kid for thee.

And the angel of the LORD said unto Manoah, Though thou detain me, I will not eat of thy bread: and if thou wilt offer a burnt offering, thou must offer it unto the LORD. FOR MANOAH KNEW NOT THAT HE WAS AN ANGEL OF THE LORD.

And Manoah said unto the angel of the LORD, What is thy name, that when thy sayings come to pass we may do thee honour?

And the angel of the LORD said unto him, Why askest thou thus after my name, seeing it is secret?

So Manoah took a kid with a meat offering, and offered it upon a rock unto the LORD: and the angel did wondrously; and Manoah and his wife looked on.

For it came to pass, when the flame went up toward heaven from off the altar, that the angel of the LORD ascended in the flame of the altar. And Manoah and his wife looked on it, and fell on their faces to the ground.

Judges 13:15-20

3. The greatest barrier to the supernatural is being "natural".

Surprisingly, the greatest barrier to the supernatural is not demons. The greatest hindrance to receiving the supernatural is not witchcraft power. *It is a state of naturalness!*

But THE NATURAL MAN RECEIVETH NOT THE THINGS OF THE SPIRIT OF GOD: for they are foolishness unto him: neither can he know them, because they are spiritually discerned.

1 Corinthians 2:14

The Bible states in very clear terms, that the *natural* man cannot receive the things of the Holy Spirit. This is because "they are foolishness unto him". What does it mean to be natural? To be natural means to be a normal human being. It speaks of thinking normally, as a human being should. To be natural is to be logical, intelligent, calculating and analytical. The word natural speaks of employing all normal human faculties. Amazingly, it is a "natural" attitude and not a "demonic" attitude that cuts you off from supernatural things.

I Could Not Receive Because of My Naturalness

Many years ago, I was desirous of receiving the Holy Spirit baptism. I wanted to experience the Holy Spirit baptism with the evidence of speaking in tongues like everybody else. Speaking in tongues is a very supernatural thing.

I remember once going to a meeting where people were being prayed for to receive the Holy Spirit. As I looked on, I began to laugh at the people. Hearing them speaking in tongues, made me laugh uncontrollably. It sounded so ridiculous. I laughed so hard that I thought I had sinned against the Holy Spirit.

Later that year, I finally decided that the baptism of the Holy Spirit was for me! I told a few people that I knew someone in town who could pray for us to receive the Holy Spirit. I remember travelling all the way into town to locate a brother who agreed to come and pray for us.

One Saturday this minister decided to attend our meeting and pray for us. As we gathered in the classroom, I was very hopeful and expectant. After preaching about the baptism of the Holy Spirit this brother prayed for everyone. He asked those who had received the Holy Spirit to raise up their hands. Then I realized that almost everybody had received, except me!

I couldn't believe it! I thought to myself, "I organized this meeting. I brought this man from town to pray for us. Yet others who have no interest in the Holy Spirit have received." I just couldn't understand it. To my left and to my right, people were speaking in tongues but I couldn't. I was very discouraged. The man of God encouraged those of us who had not received to continue praying for the Holy Spirit. I continued praying for the Holy Spirit for several weeks.

One morning, six weeks later, while lying on my bed, I routinely asked the Lord to fill me with His Holy Spirit. Before I realized it, I heard a beautiful language coming out of my spirit. I was speaking in tongues! I was so happy that I didn't stop praying in tongues for three hours. I was afraid that the Holy Spirit would go away if I stopped praying.

The question is: "Why did it take me six weeks before I received the Holy Spirit?" The answer is in the Bible: the natural man receiveth not! If you are very logical, critical, analytical, fleshly and judgemental, you are being natural. When you are natural, you will not and cannot receive spiritual things.

The Bible says that supernatural things are foolishness to people who are natural and fleshly.

4. The key to the supernatural is spiritual maturity.

And I, brethren, could not speak unto you as unto spiritual, but as unto carnal, even as unto babes in Christ.

1 Corinthians 3:1

You may have thought that people who believe in supernatural things are immature, childish and emotional. On the contrary the opposite of being natural is being spiritual. A truly mature Christian is a spiritual person and a supernatural person. A mature person knows God and God is a supernatural God. I'm not talking about academic knowledge of the Bible. Academic knowledge of the Bible does not make you spiritual. As you know, many people study Bible Knowledge and Religious Studies in school, and yet are hardened unbelievers.

In the Scripture above, the Bible declares that when people are not carnal they are spiritual.

5. The key to the supernatural is using the organs of perception.

...those who by reason of use have their SENSES EXERCISED TO DISCERN both good and evil.

Hebrews 5:14

The book of Hebrews explains that mature Christians are those who have their senses exercised to discern or distinguish good from evil.

I have always wondered what this verse meant. One of the laws of interpretation of the Bible is simply to accept the literal meaning of the words you read. This verse simply says that

28

Christians who become mature have their senses alert. The word "senses" is derived from the Greek word, aistheterion, meaning "organs of perception".

God has given you organs of perception. You are expected to use these organs of perception to maneuver in this life. Here, the Bible is giving us an additional but very important revelation. It is telling us that these organs of perception can also be used to detect or discern spiritual things. Therefore, some of your thoughts or feelings are actually supernatural things. If your heart is hardened, you will never be able to distinguish between natural and supernatural thoughts, feelings or sensations that you have. If you are not mature you will see but you will not recognize! You will hear but you will not interpret right! You will feel but you may even think that you are walking in carnality.

A young man walking in naturalness may see a lady and think he is attracted to her. Another person who is sensitive to the Holy Spirit will recognize that his attraction is actually a revelation that he is looking at a "strange and evil woman". Men who are not sensitive to the Spirit may actually go ahead and marry the very person whom the Spirit is warning them about!

When Samuel was a young man, he thought the voice he was hearing was the voice of a man. But when he matured spiritually and had a bit of training, he knew that the voice of the man was actually the voice of the Spirit.

Notice what Jesus said about people's eyes and ears. He said they could see but they were not really seeing. He said they could hear but they were not really hearing!

What Jesus Said about Organs of Perception

What are the organs of perception? They are the eyes to see, the ears to hear, the nose to smell, the skin to feel and the tongue to taste. If we accept this Scripture at face value, then it is telling us that our eyes and ears can be used, if they are spiritual, to discern between good and evil things.

Therefore speak I to them in parables: because they seeing see not; and hearing they hear not, neither do they understand.

And in them is fulfilled the prophecy of Esaias, which saith, by hearing ye shall hear, and shall not understand; and seeing ye shall see, and shall not perceive:

For this people's heart is waxed gross, and their ears are dull of hearing, and their eyes they have closed; lest at any time they should see with their eyes, and hear with their ears, and should understand with their heart, and should be converted, and I should heal them. But BLESSED ARE YOUR EYES, for they see: AND YOUR EARS, for they hear.

For verily I say unto you, That many prophets and righteous men have desired to see those things which ye see, and have not seen them; and to hear those things which ye hear, and have not heard them.

Matthew 13:13-17

Jesus made many astounding statements. He said, "Blessed are your eyes and your ears." What does this mean? *Jesus was speaking about their organs of perception, (aistheterion).*

Jesus had just finished teaching them the Word of God yet many could not understand what He was saying.

When He said, "blessed are your eyes" He meant blessed are your eyes because they see visions, revelations and the supernatural. When He said, "blessed are your ears" He meant that they heard a little further. Perhaps they were hearing the voice of the Holy Spirit and the voice of God. Some could even hear the voices of angels!

At another point in the passage, Jesus said that the people had waxed gross in their heart. The word "heart" comes from the Greek word, "*kardia*", meaning thoughts and feelings. Their thoughts and feelings, which were organs of perception, had become gross (dull, stupid, fat and inattentive).

The Supernatural Moves through Your Organs of Perception

This is the principal revelation I want you to understand. *The supernatural operates through your eyes, ears, thoughts and feelings.*

Some of the thoughts that flash in your mind are from God. They are the voice of God ministering direction to you. Jesus made it clear that the Holy Spirit would minister to Christians through their minds.

But the Comforter, which is the Holy Ghost, whom the Father will send in my name, he shall teach you all things, and BRING ALL THINGS TO YOUR REMEMBRANCE [mind], whatsoever I have said unto you.

John 14:26

"God Spoke to Me..."

This Scripture is saying that the Holy Spirit brings things to your mind. You might have heard great men of God say, "God spoke to me", or some mighty evangelists say, "The Spirit of God said something to me last night." I am sure you have wondered, as I did, that God seems to physically "live" in the houses of these men of God. God seems to speak to them all the time, but never to me. They always say, "God spoke to me."

But Jesus said that the Holy Spirit would bring things to your mind. However, if your heart (kardia - thoughts and feelings) has waxed gross (fat, stupid, dull and inattentive) you will never know when the Holy Spirit speaks into your mind. You will not know the difference between your own thoughts and those from the Holy Spirit.

6. You will miss the supernatural if you only look for the spectacular.

Learn something right here! The supernatural is not always sensational, dramatic or spectacular. The supernatural concerns things that are not natural. My experience in the supernatural is that God uses my organs of perception, of feeling, thinking, seeing and hearing. He will do the same for you. It may not be spectacular or thrilling, but it certainly is supernatural.

The supernatural is often mistaken for the natural. Because of that, the supernatural passes us by and we do not even realize it. Do you remember the call of the Prophet Samuel?

The boy Samuel was in the temple of God ministering. After lying down to sleep one night, he heard a voice. The voice sounded so much like the voice of his senior pastor that he immediately got up and went to see Pastor Eli. The prophet Eli said, "I didn't call you, so go back." He heard this same supernatural voice three times and thought he was hearing a human voice.

> **...Samuel was laid down to sleep; That the Lord called Samuel: and he answered, Here am I. And the Lord called yet again, Samuel... And the Lord called Samuel again the third time...**
>
> **1 Samuel 3:3-4, 6, 8**

If the supernatural voice were not similar to a natural voice, then why would Samuel make the same mistake three times? It was the experienced prophet, Eli, who guided Samuel to receiving the supernatural.

> **Therefore Eli said unto Samuel, Go, lie down: and it shall be, if he call thee, that thou shalt say, Speak, Lord; for thy servant heareth. So Samuel went and lay down in his place. And the Lord came, and stood, and called as at other times, Samuel, Samuel. Then Samuel answered, Speak, for thy servant heareth.**
>
> **1 Samuel 3:9, 10**

7. Many are called in an ordinary way, few are called in a spectacular way, but all are called in a supernatural way.

For MANY ARE CALLED, but few are chosen.
Matthew 22:14

The call of God on my life has simply been a conviction. A conviction to serve Him. A conviction to do my best. A conviction to obey the desires that He has placed on my heart. The Bible is true when it says many are called. Many, many, many people are called.

I have been in the ministry for many years. God has used me to do many things for which I am grateful. For example, you are reading a book that I have written. That alone should tell you that God is using me to some extent. However, I did not experience thundering and lightning and I have not seen Jesus in person. But I believe I have a very supernatural ministry.

The things I do and have been able to accomplish have been divinely and supernaturally orchestrated.

Many people do not respect the visions they see. Many have had dreams, which they take no notice of. Paul said, I was obedient to the heavenly vision. One night, God spoke to me and told me, "Respect your dreams." I told the Lord, "But I don't have spectacular dreams!"

The Lord told me to look in the book of Daniel. So I opened my Bible and He showed me that even King Nebuchadnezzer, an unbeliever, respected his dreams greatly. As a result, he was able to receive an instruction from the Lord.

His dream revealed a mighty tree being cut down. If you had a dream where you just saw a tree, would you take much notice of it? Probably not! You may take more notice of a dream where cows were chasing you, birds were flying, and snakes were appearing all over the place.

How did Elijah experience the supernatural? He experienced the supernatural through a still small voice. God was not in the earthquake, wind or fire.

And he said, Go forth, and stand upon the mount before the Lord. And, behold, the Lord passed by, and a great and strong wind rent the mountains, and brake in pieces the rocks before the Lord; but the Lord was not in the wind: and after the wind an earthquake; but the Lord was not in the earthquake: And after the earthquake a fire; but the Lord was not in the fire: and after the fire A STILL SMALL VOICE.

1 Kings 19:11, 12

CHAPTER 4

How to Cooperate with the Supernatural

And a certain man was there, which had an infirmity thirty and eight years. When Jesus saw him lie, and knew that he had been now a long time in that case, he saith unto him, Wilt thou be made whole?

The impotent man answered him, Sir, I have no man, when the water is troubled, to put me into the pool: but while I am coming, another steppeth down before me.

Jesus saith unto him, Rise, take up thy bed, and walk. And immediately the man was made whole, and took up his bed, and walked: and on the same day was the sabbath.

John 5:5-9

The story of the healing of the paralytic proves to us that Jesus did not attempt to do supernatural things unless He saw that God was doing them.

Jesus went to the Pool of Bethesda and met a man who had been there for thirty-eight years. This man had been at the pool for such a long time because he did not have any nurses to help him.

I once saw a similar situation in a hospital. There was a man who had an accident that broke his hip joint such that he couldn't walk. He needed to have surgery but this man didn't know anybody who could help him. He was not a rich man. He was also not an important person. So every time he was scheduled for surgery, somebody else was given his place. This man continued to lie in bed even though his case needed immediate surgery! Eventually, one year later, he had his surgery which was too late to be effective.

He was just like the man by the pool of Bethesda who had no one to help him. Jesus selected this man for healing and ignored all the others. There was a large number of very ill people there. Would He heal all of them? Did He heal all of them? Did He attempt to line them up and minister to them? The answer is "no". Jesus simply ignored the large number of sick people around Him and ministered to one person.

Why did Jesus heal only one person? How did He select this man out of the crowd? He followed the visible appearance of the Holy Spirit. Jesus did not talk to any of the sick people. Seeing this man and suddenly knowing a little about his condition made him sense that God was interested in that man. We would probably say that Jesus had a "word of knowledge" about that man.

The unspiritual and faithless would say that Jesus just healed the first person He saw. However, the spiritual person does not operate by chance, by luck or by good fortune. He knows that God is at work even in his thoughts.

As soon as Jesus saw and knew something about this man, He believed that God was leading Him to help that man.

Six Keys to Cooperating with the Supernatural

1. **Work only when you see the Father working.**

    But Jesus answered them, My Father worketh hitherto, and I work.

    John 5:17

The key to aligning yourself with God is following the Holy Spirit. The key to following the Holy Spirit is to watch what He is doing and where He is doing it. In other words, Jesus was saying, "If I see my Father working, I will jump in and work. If I see my Father ministering to someone, then I will minister to him."

Then answered Jesus and said unto them, Verily, verily, I say unto you, The Son can do nothing of himself, but what he seeth the Father do: for what things soever he doeth, these also doeth the Son likewise.

John 5:19

Jesus restricted His ministration to what He could see the Father doing. Unlike some of us, who want to pray for everyone and heal everyone, Jesus restricted Himself to doing only what His Father did. Jesus knew that He could fulfil the purposes of God better by restricting His activities to what the Father did.

Jesus did not feel embarrassed that only one person would be healed. Jesus was not embarrassed by the fact that people would think, "There were not many miracles today." Jesus did not care whether people thought He was powerful or not. If His Father wanted one miracle, He would do no more than one miracle.

2. Wait until you see the Father working.

For the Father loveth the Son, and sheweth him all things that himself doeth: and he will shew him greater works than these, that ye may marvel.

John 5:20

Be patient! Don't rush! I must wait till I see my Father showing me His miracles and His works. When God loves you, He will show you what He is doing. When God loves you, He will show you whom He is healing and whom He is touching. If you do not wait to see what the Father is doing, you will stumble in the dark and experiment with unworkable things.

Occasionally, you will find something that works. But most of the time, you will be found beating the air and sweating away to no purpose.

You cannot do anything until God does it. If He is not making your church grow you cannot make it grow yourself. If He is not healing you, you cannot be healed.   If He is not delivering you, you cannot be delivered. God doesn't just do everything for everybody.

God is always doing something in particular. We must wait and see what God is doing. We must be patient! We must flow with what He is doing. We must move away from what He is not doing!

3. Accept and follow the manifestations of healings.

Healings are a special manifestation of the Spirit. It is the manifestation that marks out the new covenant. People can fake crying, screaming, shaking and trembling. But, no man can fake healings. People are either healed or they are not. Following the visible appearance of the Spirit is the great key to a successful healing ministry: Follow the visible appearances of the Holy Spirit. This is the key to the healing ministry: pray for those that God is healing. Avoid praying for people that God is not healing. All your past failures in ministry can be attributed to your doing things that God was not doing. Every time we pray for someone whom God is not touching, there is an impression that God's power is not there. There is a feeling that there is no anointing. The most successful ministers are those who strictly follow the Holy Spirit.

I remember praying for a twenty-five-year old lady who was dying in hospital. I knew that God loved her and would never let her die at that age. Unfortunately, she did die in spite of my strong and fervent prayers for her. This was a confusing experience for me because this lady was a faithful long-standing Christian who loved God with all her might. Yet she died in the prime of her life, leaving behind a husband and a child.

Why does God do apparently insignificant miracles in a miracle service when there are really ill people who need healing badly? It is these looming questions that caused many of the great healing evangelists to question the healing ministry and eventually stop ministering healing.

4. Accept and follow all of the eighteen manifestations of the Spirit.

The key to successfully ministering the Spirit is to watch out for what God is doing. If you can see that God is touching someone visibly, then you simply also touch the person. You must accept when God is ministering to someone who begins shaking, trembling, screaming or crying! Notice if people are being healed! Notice if people are falling under the power! Notice if there are prophecies! If the Spirit shows you that He is touching someone, touch that person. Leave all the other dry bones! This is the great key to successfully ministering the Spirit.

It is important to accept what God is doing and flow with it. If you flow with the move of God, He will be with you. If you fight against what He is doing you will never succeed. After years of walking with the Lord, I have simply lost all confidence in my ability to do my own thing. I just have to trust Him and do what He wants to do. Ultimately, we belong to God. We can only do what He is doing.

But speaking the truth in love, may grow up into him in all things, which is the head, even Christ:

Ephesians 4:15

We must grow up into Him in all things. This means that we must grow up in healings, miracles and manifestations of the Holy Spirit. We must grow up in our understanding of the administration of the Spirit. We must grow up in Him in the workings and the moves of the Spirit.

5. Accept and follow men whom the Spirit is using.

Unfortunately, the Lord is not as predictable as we would like Him to be. Human beings love predictable things. We want to be able to say, "This is what God will do!" We want to be able to say, "God will heal this person tomorrow." We wish we could predict whether God will use this young man and not the other one. However, most of the time we are wrong. God does not fit into our stereotypes.

You can never tell whom God is going to use. You can hardly tell whether God is going to heal someone or not. It is very difficult to tell whether this person will live long or not. No one can tell if God will use the pastor's son or a stranger from nowhere.

I have seen large families, in which the parents predicted which of their sons would be a priest. They also predicted which son would be a wicked businessman. Surprisingly, the wicked man turned out to be the priest and the priest turned out to be something else.

As it is written, Jacob have I loved, but Esau have I hated.

Romans 9:13

This is a Scripture that confuses many people. We wrestle with the fact that God would choose a thief and a trickster. Why would God leave the decent firstborn son, who pleased his father and replace him with this con man?

Align Yourself with God

God cannot be predicted and stereotyped! What we need to know and understand is: "What is God doing at this particular moment?" This is often different from what we expect God to do. There will be more miracles, more successes, more victories when we get to walk with God. After all, it is God who will do the work. It is God who will build the Church. It is God who will make you successful. The Bible says it clearly: the God who called you is the one who will actually do it.

Faithful is he that calleth you, who also will do it.
1 Thessalonians 5:24

6. Accept and follow what God is doing in churches.

One of the keys to successful church planting and church growth is to plant your church where God is visibly working with churches. Your new church is likely to work in a city where God is obviously working to build churches. A city in which large churches flourish is a city where the Holy Spirit is visibly causing churches to grow. A church will never grow without the power of the Holy Spirit at work.

CHAPTER 5

The Four Laws of Miracles and Manifestations

Every field of endeavour has its rules and laws. You must learn the rules of miracles and manifestations of the Spirit if you want to operate in them. The way God does things is sometimes different from the way we would like Him to.

> **For my thoughts are not your thoughts, neither are your ways my ways, saith the Lord. For as the heavens are higher than the earth, so are my ways higher than your ways, and my thoughts than your thoughts.**
>
> **Isaiah 55:8, 9**

Supernatural healing is different from natural healing. One of the biggest questions facing all miracle ministries is, "Why is everyone not healed?" Another question is: "Why do some people seem to have all the blessings and others have no blessings at all?"

The existence of these questions in your mind can keep you away from experiencing the supernatural. Please remember that there were questions in the minds of the people in Jesus' hometown. They questioned His background as well as His source of power. Generally speaking, they were questioning the validity of His ministry.

1. The Law of Divine Selection

The supernatural operates by the law of divine selection. Jesus spoke about this law in the book of Luke. He said that there were many widows in the days of Elijah the prophet; however, only one widow received a miracle. God knows about the masses of humans suffering and He cares. It seems to me that when God is ministering, He selects out of the masses and ministers to some.

There were hundreds of sick and dying lepers in the days of Naaman the Syrian. Jesus again spoke about how Naaman was divinely selected for a miracle.

But I tell you of a truth, many widows were in Israel in the days of Elias, when the heaven was shut up three years and six months, when great famine was throughout all the land; But unto none of them was Elias sent, save unto Sarepta, a city of Sidon, unto a woman that was a widow.

And many lepers were in Israel in the time of Eliseus the prophet; and none of them was cleansed, saving Naaman the Syrian.

Luke 4:25-27

It is by this same principle that the man at the Pool of Bethesda was healed. Some people may say it was because of his faith. Others may say it was because of the anointing on the man of God. I would simply say that there is a law of divine selection. We do not understand everything. Nobody does! The Bible says that we are looking through a glass dimly. We neither see nor know everything!

For now WE SEE THROUGH A GLASS, DARKLY; but then face to face: now I know in part; but then shall I know even as also I am known.

1 Corinthians 13:12

"Why then do pastors preach as if everyone is going to be healed?" People ask, "Why do evangelists raise hopes when people may not get healed?"

Dear friend, there is no other way to raise up the faith of people except you stand boldly and speak in faith. Any pastor who begins his sermon by saying, "Some will not be blessed in this miracle service," is not raising up the faith of the people.

If you want miracles, you have to preach faith. If you want the power of God, you have to preach about the power of God. Jesus preached about the anointing. He said, "The spirit of the Lord is upon me." He spoke about how God had anointed him. When you preach about the anointing, the anointing will flow. When you talk about healing, healing will happen. Faith comes by hearing and hearing by the Word. When you preach doubt you will get nothing.

So then faith cometh by hearing, and hearing by the word of God.

Romans 10:17

As a pastor, I pray for miracles and breakthroughs for my people. I once prayed for a group of ladies who had not been able to have children. Some of them became pregnant and had children. I prayed again and again for some of them but they were still not able to have children. Surprisingly, some who already had children were blessed with even more children.

I would ask myself, "Oh God! Why don't you share this thing evenly? So many don't have any children at all. Why don't you answer our prayers and give everybody at least one child?" Jesus made it very clear in his sermon. There are many sick people like Naaman, who need help. There are many more poor people like the widow of Sarepta, who need a financial miracle. But God will have his own way of ministering to them.

When it comes to the supernatural move of the Holy Spirit, you can often not tell what God will do. We do know that He will do something. But we do not always know whom He will do it for and why He will do it.

2. The Law of Humility

The woman with the issue of blood had been through many things.

And a certain woman, which had an issue of blood twelve years, And had SUFFERED MANY THINGS of many physicians, and had spent all that she had, and was nothing bettered, but rather grew worse,

Mark 5:25, 26

She had been bleeding for twelve years. She had suffered at the hands of several doctors. She had been humiliated time and time again in different hospitals.

By the time this woman came to Jesus, she had no confidence in herself. She had no hope in man. She had no trust in human medicine. She had been completely softened by the experiences of life. This had made her humble and open to receive. God resists the proud, but He gives grace to the humble. God gives miracles and blessings to humble people.

When you are proud, you often don't know it. Experiences of life can calm you down and allow you to begin to trust in the grace of God. Don't be worried by the difficult times you are going through. Perhaps, you are on the road of humility. God is breaking down your resistance. He is causing you to be ready and open to receive grace. Your day for a miracle is around the corner.

This woman did not even want to meet Jesus. All she wanted to do was to touch the tip of His garment. That is humility indeed! Humble yourself in the sight of God and He will raise you up!

Humble yourselves therefore under the mighty hand of God, that he may exalt you in due time:

1 Peter 5:6

3. The Law of Repeated Ministrations

If God ministers to you, should you not have an instant recovery? This is what I would expect. However, there is often a need for repeated and sustained ministrations to the same person. You will see this law in operation many times in the Bible.

Why was Naaman asked to dip himself in the River Jordan seven times? He had to bathe seven different times in the same river. The question is, why not one bath? Why not three times? Why not six times? The answer is, "I don't know." God decided to bless Naaman after the seventh ministration.

And Elisha sent a messenger unto him, saying, Go and wash in Jordan seven times, and thy flesh shall come again to thee, and thou shalt be clean...Then went he down, and dipped himself SEVEN times in Jordan, according to the saying of the man of God: and his flesh came again like unto the flesh of a little child, and he was clean.

2 Kings 5:10, 14

Elijah prayed for rain seven times. On seven different occasions, he sent his assistant to look at the clouds.

...And Elijah went up to the top of Carmel; and he cast himself down upon the earth, and put his face between his knees, and said to his servant, Go up now, look toward the sea. And he went up, and looked, and said, there is nothing. And he said, Go again SEVEN TIMES.

1 Kings 18:42, 43

There was no sign of rain until after the *seventh prayer.*

...And it came to pass at the SEVENTH TIME, that he said, Behold, there ariseth a little cloud out of the sea, like a man's hand...

1 Kings 18: 44

Your miracle may appear after several ministrations. Do not be tired of being prayed for several times. Greater men had to pray seven times and were not angry with God. Please do not be angry with God because you have to pray several times for the same thing. Do not develop a bitter spirit and attitude!

When Elijah prayed for a dead boy, he had to pray *three times*.

And he stretched himself upon the child THREE TIMES, and cried unto the Lord, and said, O Lord my God, I pray thee, let this child's soul come into him again. And the Lord heard the voice of Elijah; and the soul of the child came into him again, and he revived.

1 Kings 17:21, 22

He lay on the boy three times and prayed. Is this just a mystical ritual? No it is not! It is the law of sustained and repeated ministrations at work. Do you remember when Joshua led the people of God around the walls of Jericho? They had the greatest breakthrough of their lives. But it came only after the seventh round of ministration.

And it came to pass at the SEVENTH time, when the priests blew with the trumpets, Joshua said unto the people, Shout; for the Lord hath given you the city. So the people shouted when the priests blew with the trumpets... that the wall fell down flat...

Joshua 6:16, 20

Keep up the sustained ministration. You may need to anoint someone seven times before his miracle comes.

Jesus prayed two times for a blind man.

And he cometh to Bethsaida; and they bring a blind man unto him, and besought him to touch him.

And he took the blind man by the hand, and led him out of the town; and when he had spit on his eyes, and put his hands upon him, he asked him if he saw ought. And he looked up, and said, I see men as trees, walking.

AFTER THAT HE PUT HIS HANDS AGAIN UPON HIS EYES, and made him look up: and he was restored, and saw every man clearly.

Mark 8:22-25

After the first ministration, he saw men as trees. Even Jesus had to minister a second time before the miracle finally came through. Someone may ask, "If He was truly the Son of God why did He have to pray twice?" That was the law of repeated ministration at work.

The disciples did not receive the Holy Spirit only once. In John 20:24, Jesus breathed on them and said, "Receive ye the Holy Spirit." That was their first anointing.

And when he had said this, he breathed on them, and saith unto them, RECEIVE YE THE HOLY GHOST...

John 20:22

Later on, the disciples received another baptism of the power of the Holy Spirit.

And THEY WERE FILLED WITH THE HOLY GHOST, and began to speak with other tongues, as the Spirit gave them utterance.

Acts 2:4

Yet again, they were filled with the Holy Spirit.

And when they had prayed, the place was shaken where they were assembled together; and THEY WERE ALL FILLED WITH THE HOLY GHOST, and they spake the word of God with boldness.

Acts 4:31

If the first filling was enough, then why did they have three in-fillings? This was the law of repeated ministration at work. God's power works through repeated ministrations.

4. The Law of Spiritual Timing

It is important to understand the law of the timing of miracles. Why did Jesus come -to the Earth only two thousand years ago? When the time was right, God sent His Son.

But when the fulness of the time was come, God sent forth his Son, made of a woman, made under the law,
Galatians 4:4

Jesus was a gift of God to the Jews, but in the day of their divine blessing, they did not receive the gift. It is important for you to recognize the time of your visitation. God has a time in His timetable when He is going to bless you with certain gifts.

God's Timing Is Best

In 1988, God placed me in the office of a teacher. At another time, He placed on me the anointing to pastor the church. He then gave me an anointing to minister with miracles and manifestations of the Holy Spirit. Why didn't He do it all at once? God has a time for your breakthrough. As you flow with Him, you will come into special days for your life and you will be truly blessed.

Do not be angry with God because He is keeping to His schedule! God may not come when you want Him to come. But He will come in time! Be a man or woman of spiritual understanding. You will have your miracle baby. You will have your healing. You will have your financial breakthrough. Trust in the Lord with all your heart and understand the time. When it is your time, you will walk in it and enjoy it.

For there shall come a time, saith the Lord, when you will not seek for miracles but you will seek for my wholeness. When you seek after me, I will add unto you all things that are necessary.

Fear not my little flock, for I have laid a table for you in the presence of your enemies. Do not be afraid of the enemies you see all around you.

For in that day, saith the Lord, I will pour out my anointing so strong that you will taste of my goodness and my mercies. Those that despise you will stand and declare, "The Lord has done great things for them."

CHAPTER 6

How You Can Be Anointed for Miracles and Manifestations

1. You can be anointed for miracles and manifestations by catching the anointing like Jesus Christ did.

HOW GOD ANOINTED JESUS OF NAZARETH WITH THE HOLY GHOST AND WITH POWER: who went about doing good, and healing all that were oppressed of the devil; for God was with him.
Acts 10:38

Let this mind be in you, which was also in Christ Jesus: Who, being in the form of God, thought it not robbery to be equal with God: But made himself of no reputation, and took upon him the form of a servant, and was made in the likeness of men: AND BEING FOUND IN FASHION AS A MAN, he humbled himself, and became obedient unto death, even the death of the cross.
Philippians 2:5-8

Many people do not understand that Jesus Christ, although he was the Son of God was also the Son of Man. He did that so we would realize that He had taken upon

Himself the form of a man. He humbled Himself and was "found in fashion as a man."

Becoming a man means that He had all the frailties and weaknesses of man. He was tempted in all points like we are.

For we have not an high priest which cannot be touched with the feeling of our infirmities; but was in all points tempted like as we are, yet without sin.

Hebrews 4:15

Jesus experienced all our temptations. If you have a temptation to drink, He was tempted to drink. If you have temptations to commit fornication, Jesus was tempted to commit fornication. If you are tempted to lie, He was tempted to lie. If you are tempted to steal, He was tempted to steal. If you are tempted to bear a grudge against someone, Jesus was tempted many times to hold a grudge against the people who persecuted Him. If you are tempted to be afraid, He was too. He was tempted to be afraid of going to the cross and to face all the wicked people. He was tempted because He was a normal human being.

He is the greatest example for all of us. We are not following someone that cannot be followed. We can follow Him because He became like we are. He had the weaknesses that we have because all men are imperfect. This is why He had to pray like we do. If he were God on Earth, He wouldn't have needed to pray.

The big question is, "How was a man able to do the miracles that He did? How was He able to raise the dead? How was He able to call back to life a man who had been dead for four days, and whose body had decomposed? How was He able to call a man out of his coffin and make him come alive again? How was He able to heal blind people? How come people who were suffering from certain diseases were healed?"

We can find the answer in the Bible. We learn how God anointed Jesus Christ of Nazareth with the Holy Spirit and with power. That was when He went about doing good and healing all that were oppressed of the devil. Jesus was able to do miracles because of the anointing that was put on Him by the Father.

God anointed Jesus with the power to cast out devils and the power to break the yoke of the enemy. Jesus, who was now in the form of a servant, was a special servant because He was an anointed servant and an anointed man.

Many people think that Jesus was called Jesus Christ because His surname was Christ. They think that He was the son of Mr. and Mrs. Joseph and Mary Christ. That is not the case. Jesus was known as Jesus of Nazareth but He was actually given a nickname, "Christ", which means "the Anointed One." This was because He was so associated with the presence of GOD and the anointing.

This anointing explains the miracles that Jesus did. It explains why Jesus Christ, although he took on the form of man, was able to do great things. He went about doing good! What were the good things that Jesus did? The good things were, healing suffering people who were oppressed by the devil. Jesus the man was now the anointed man. We have hope that just as God anointed Jesus, He will also anoint us!

When you recognize that the secret behind the miracles is the anointing, you will not be interested in the man of God's car, house, educational background, wife or his money but in the anointing that is upon his life.

The good things that Jesus did are the good things that God is calling us to do. It is good to build schools and provide social amenities but the good works that Jesus did were preaching the gospel, healing the sick, casting out devils, raising the dead and cleansing the lepers.

Elisha Recognized the Need to Catch the Anointing from Elijah

Elijah lived with Elisha for many years. At the end of Elijah's life, he asked him, "My son, what would you like me to leave you when I die? Do you want my house? I've got three houses down in Bethel. I've got a house in Jericho. I've got a house down here and houses all over town."

Elisha said, "I don't want your house."

Elijah asked Elisha, "What would you like to have? I've got some land in Bethlehem, and another plot in Jericho."

But Elisha said, "I don't want your land."

He asked again, "Do you like my donkeys? I have 27 donkeys which travel all over the world. Do you like my cars?"

But Elisha was too wise for that. He said, "I don't like your donkeys. I don't want your cars. I don't want anything from you. All I want is the anointing that you have. I can see that the secret behind your ministry is the anointing."

Elisha said, "All I want is the anointing. Touch me with the anointing. Let me have two times the anointing that you have. Keep your cars, keep your donkeys, keep your houses, but give me the anointing!"

Many people don't know that the secret behind the blessing of the Lord is the anointing. When Jesus lowered Himself and became a man, born of a peasant woman, into a carpenter's house and under questionable circumstances. He seemed very lowly. But the anointing makes all the difference! I see the anointing making the difference in your life!

I want you to understand that the anointing is the most important thing that you must seek for. It takes a lot to be anointed. When Elisha asked Elijah for his anointing, Elijah said, "You have asked for a hard thing."

And it came to pass, when they were gone over, that Elijah said unto Elisha, Ask what I shall do for thee, before I be taken away from thee. And Elisha said, I pray thee, let a double portion of thy spirit be upon me. And he said, THOU HAST ASKED A HARD THING: nevertheless, if thou see me when I am taken from thee, it shall be so unto thee; but if not, it shall not be so.
2 Kings 2:9-10

It is not easy to be anointed. You may go to school but not become anointed. You may be qualified from a Bible school but still not be anointed. You may read books but still not be anointed.

The Apostle Paul was anointed. He said, "He that hath anointed us is God."

Now he which stablisheth us with you in Christ, and hath anointed us, is God;

2 Corinthians 1:21

The anointing is what makes the difference in the life of every minister. It was the anointing that made the difference in the life of Jesus.

How I Caught the Anointing

I must be anointed otherwise you will not be reading this book. When I started teaching in the Ministry, I didn't know what the anointing was. You don't need to understand how the anointing works to enjoy it. Many of us do not understand how the television works, yet we use it.

I started out by preaching and teaching without the anointing. But there is a difference between a schoolteacher and an anointed pastor. A schoolteacher teaches and a pastor also teaches but the difference is the anointing.

I had started a little church and had been preaching for some years as a medical student. Sometime in 1988, I had to fulfil what is called a community health rotation. Every class in medical school is divided into groups. Each group rotated through different fields of medicine throughout the year. That is why it was called a rotation. I had to complete four rotations in my final year, one each for surgery, medicine, specials and community health.

During the community health rotation, I had to travel outside the capital city to a smaller town called Suhum, in another region of Ghana. I lived in the Suhum Government Hospital for one month. I was to gain practical experience in running a hospital and working out on the field where conditions are different from the bigger cities.

Although I was fulfilling my medical requirements, as usual my mind was on the ministry. By the second week, I took advantage of a more relaxed timetable and decided to fast and pray. On my way out of Accra to Suhum, I had passed through a Christian bookshop and bought some Kenneth Hagin tapes. I felt I would need something to "soak in" whilst I was in Suhum. I had been a great follower and admirer of Kenneth Hagin's ministry. Actually, I had already listened to those tapes many times but I thought I just needed something nice to listen to.

The Night of the Anointing

One night, I was praying, fasting and listening to one of these tapes that I had bought. At about 3 a.m. in the morning I was kneeling by the bed praying. I could see the tape recorder situated at the other end of the room. Then suddenly, something literally jumped out of the tape that was playing and entered into my belly. I could feel it entering me. Then I heard a voice saying, "From now you can teach." I didn't know what that was but I thought to myself, "That's good, because I want to teach." I didn't know at that time that I had received a major impartation of the anointing.

At that time, my church comprised of about twenty-five students. The Bible teaches that we should prove all things, so I decided to try out this new gifting. I was invited to teach at a Full Gospel Businessmen's breakfast meeting in Suhum. This was my first opportunity to preach after my impartation experience. I tell you, I noticed a difference! After the ministration someone asked me where my church was. He was surprised that I was an unknown minister. Within me, I knew that something had happened that was making a difference.

When I got back to the church after a month, I noticed a difference in my ability to teach and preach. The anointing had arrived and I began to build up. The first series I preached was about the prodigal son. I preached this on a weekday and the attendance and interest in the service began to increase steadily. I noticed there was some life and Spirit in my ministry. It is difficult to describe it but when it's there you know it's there!

The anointing is a bit like beauty - when you see it, you know it! You can't easily explain how or why you recognize a beautiful lady. But when you see someone beautiful you know it. I have no reason to share what I am sharing except to help you. My ministry has grown in leaps and bounds because of the anointing. It is the anointing that changes you from a normal person to a super normal person. I see that anointing coming upon your life!!!

The Lord anointed me that night to teach. Since then I've been teaching and preaching. The anointing that the Lord gave me is similar to the one through whom I received the anointing and that's why I've written a number of books. It is the anointing that we need. It is not cleverness. It is the anointing that makes the difference.

The Anointing Makes You into a Different Person

God anointed Jesus with the Holy Spirit and with power. This is what made Him do the miracles that He did. We cannot preach about Jesus without talking about miracles. There are miracles from the beginning of the Bible. When the anointing is on your life, you're a different person. People would like to remind you of the old times and say that you are still a nobody. But when the anointing is on you, you are "another man".

You may be known as a thief today but one day, you'll be known as an anointed person. The anointing changes you and makes you into a miracle worker. It changes you into a supernatural person.

2. **You can be anointed for miracles and manifestations by being humble.**

   Now when all the people were baptized, it came to pass, that Jesus also being baptized, and praying, the heaven was opened, And the Holy Spirit descended in a bodily shape like a dove upon him, and a voice came from heaven, which said, Thou art my beloved Son; in thee I am well pleased.

   Luke 3:21-22

   Jesus submitted Himself to John the Baptist even though He was God. God will anoint someone who is humble enough to submit Himself to another.

   There are many rebellious elements in the church who are looking for the anointing. They are looking for God's gifts but God does not anoint illegal things. That is why everyone that uses the name of Christ must depart from iniquity. God anoints people who love righteousness and hate iniquity. "Thou hast loved righteousness, and hated iniquity; therefore God, even thy God, hath anointed thee with the oil of gladness above thy fellows" (Hebrews 1:9).

   Nevertheless the foundation of God standeth sure, having this seal, The Lord knoweth them that are his. And, LET EVERY ONE THAT NAMETH THE NAME OF CHRIST DEPART FROM INIQUITY.

   2 Timothy 2:19

   God doesn't just anoint anyone. Today, you can see ministers fighting with everyone who was there before them. Yet you can see Jesus Christ humbling and submitting Himself to the person who was there before Him. Why are you so different from Jesus Christ? Do you think you will ever be as anointed as He was?

Humility Pleases God

Notice that before Jesus had the chance to preach one sermon or to heal one person, a voice came from Heaven saying, "This is my beloved Son." If you really want to please God just humble yourself like Jesus did. The fall of Satan was caused by pride. The same thing has caused every other fall since then.

I remember talking to a Bishop who used to be the general superintendent of a large denomination. He said that in his term of office as the superintendent, he had dealt with one thousand and five hundred pastors who fell into various difficulties and problems. He remarked that the one common factor in all the one thousand five hundred cases was pride. Is that not surprising?

If you want to be great in the house of God, be humble! Jesus told us who would be the greatest in the Kingdom.

Therefore whoever humbles himself as this little child is the greatest in the kingdom of heaven.
Matthew 18:4

If you become as humble as a child, you will be the greatest in the Kingdom. That is why the Son of God went forward to be baptized like everyone else. He did not ask to be treated specially. "Humble yourselves in the sight of the Lord and he shall lift you up" (James 4:10).

God is playing musical chairs with you. If you sit on the chair, he will stand, and if you stand, he will sit. If you choose to humble yourself, He will exalt you but if you choose to exalt yourself, then He will bring you down. You have to choose.

I Had to Be Humble

When the Lord called me into the Ministry and I started out in obedience, one day my father said to me, "I cannot stand the fact that my son will live from collections or offerings of people. It is below you." But the Lord told me to enter into ministry and to humble myself. I struggled with this because I was a doctor. I argued that I did not need the coins and little contributions of people to take care of myself. I did not want people to look at me and pass comments about me using the church's money.

So I told the Lord, "I cannot do this," and the Lord said to me, "You are nothing, you are nobody!"

That is true because we are all nothing. Maybe you haven't been to the mortuary before. In the mortuary, you will realize that you are nothing. If you die right now, you will be surprised to find yourself lying amongst a heap of other dead people you do not know.

We are what we are by the grace of God. That's why we should humble ourselves in the sight of the Lord and allow him to lift us up. This is exactly what Jesus did when He came down to earth. He didn't want to be exalted.

Jesus became anointed because He humbled Himself! He joined the masses for baptism. Stop trying to be special. Stop trying to be different. Stop trying to be some unique person. Just become nothing. When you humble yourself God will pour His grace on you. If you do not humble yourself, you cannot learn and receive from the people that God sends to you. You will analyse them instead of receiving from them. Many of us are outside the grace of God because we can't receive from the people that God has put in our lives.

This is what happens in the Church. When God sends people into our lives, we cannot receive from them because we are not able to humble ourselves. It is only because Jesus humbled Himself before John the Baptist that God anointed Him. That was the hour that the Holy Spirit came upon Him. The anointing flows downwards to people who are positioned below in humility.

It is like the precious ointment upon the head, that ran down upon the beard, even Aaron's beard: that went down to the skirts of his garments;

Psalm 133:2

The anointing can only come on you when you're lowly. Humble yourself in the sight of the Lord. The way up is the way down. The way high is the way low. I see the Lord anointing you!

3. **You can be anointed for miracles and manifestations through prayer.**

Now when all the people were baptized, it came to pass, that JESUS ALSO BEING BAPTIZED, AND PRAYING, the heaven was opened,

Luke 3:21

You must note that the anointing came upon Jesus when he was praying. There is no anointing without prayer. Prayerless people are powerless people. Prayer is what gives rise to the intangible aura around anointed people.

Someone would wonder why the Pharisees were afraid to arrest Jesus. He had preached openly. He had been in the temple, casting out thieves. He had marched into Jerusalem on a donkey. Jesus moved around openly. Why were they afraid to arrest Him? Why did they need Judas to betray someone who walked around openly in public? It is because there was an aura around Jesus. There was something about Him. There was something about His words. His words have lasted for more than two thousand years. He never wrote a book but two thousand years later, millions read His words.

When His disciples noticed this intangible aura, they asked Him, "Teach us how to pray." They did not ask Him to teach them how to preach or how to become anointed.

And it came to pass, that, as he was praying in a certain place, when he ceased, one of his disciples said unto him, Lord, teach us to pray, as John also taught his disciples.

Luke 11:1

Authority Comes from the Anointing

You see, when you have been with someone, you can speak about the person with authority. The authority comes because you have been with the person. This authority is a manifestation of the anointing on your life. The more anointed you are, the more authority you will have. And the more authority you have, the more powerful you will be. Some years ago, our church had a problem with the government. Our church had been vandalized and we needed some help. We needed to get close to the highest authority of the land, so we found someone whom we knew was close to the President. I remember going to his house to explain the problem to him. I remember that every time I saw him in his house, there was an aura of importance around him because this person was always with the President.

Sometimes, we had to wait for him in his house till he would come and meet with us. We always knew that he had been with the President. We took our files to him and when he asked us to leave the matter with him, we expected that he would be able to see the President and do something about the problem. We believed everything he told us because we knew that he had power. We knew he was close to the real source of power. We were attracted to him because of his authority.

Although he never really helped us, we kept on going there because of his authority and the fact that he was always with the President. It was not his physical strength that attracted us to him. We went to him because he was close to the President.

People received Jesus Christ because they could tell that He had been with the highest of powers. They knew that He had been with the Almighty El-Shaddai. They knew that He had been with Jehovah Rophe. The presence of the Lord around Him came from the fact that He had spoken to the Lord. That presence and the aura that is around you after prayer is a manifestation of the anointing. The anointing for miracles and manifestations of power is found on prayerful people.

4. **You can be anointed for miracles and manifestations by waiting for your season.**

    AND JESUS HIMSELF BEGAN TO BE ABOUT THIRTY YEARS OF AGE, being (as was supposed) the son of Joseph, which was the son of Heli,

    Luke 3:23

Why was Jesus anointed when He was thirty years old? Why was Jesus not anointed earlier?

We have not received certain things because we are not yet "thirty years" of age. We have not received certain things because we are not yet the right age for them. Jesus began to enter into the blessings that had been determined for Him when he was thirty years old. There is a time for certain experiences. The Bible talks about a tree bringing forth fruit in its season.

And he shall be like a tree planted by the rivers of water, that bringeth forth his fruit in his season; his leaf also shall not wither; and whatsoever he doeth shall prosper.

Psalm 1:3

John the Baptist was about thirty years old when he began his ministry. The priests that did the work of the Lord were those who were thirty years old and above.

Now the Levites were numbered from the age of thirty years and upward:

1 Chronicles 23:3

David began to reign when he was thirty years old.

David was thirty years old when he began to reign, and he reigned forty years.

2 Samuel 5:4

There is a season for everything that God has planned for your life. Be patient and wait for Him. When it's the season for your anointing, it will surely arrive. There will be no delay. Pray and cry no more. Don't think that you have done something wrong.

There is a season for your breakthrough. There is a time for God to lift you up. Enter into your season of lifting. The season of blessing, the season of healing and the season of promotion shall come at the right time! I see you entering into the season of God for your life!

The mother of John the Baptist had to wait for her son to arrive at the right season. John the Baptist had to be born a few months before Christ was born so that he could prepare the way for Jesus' Ministry. That was God's season for him. He could not have come earlier, or later. Elizabeth simply had to wait for the right season to have her child.

Until you begin to be about "thirty years", nothing will happen. If you are a pastor, don't give up. The time for your anointing and breakthrough is coming. Your time will come as surely as the night follows the day. It will come at the season that God has determined for it. When it's the rainy season, you don't have to call for the rain. You won't need to fast and pray for the rain. The rain will pour on you because its season has come.

A Megachurch at the Right Season

Years ago, I preached mainly to small groups. I began to complain to the Lord that I had never preached to a large group of people. I said to the Lord, "Why is it that I am starting little groups which never became large?" The Lord told me not to give up. He promised me that there was a megachurch down the line for me. At the right time and at the right season, I began to see the megachurch the Lord had promised.

You are just about to enter into your season! You are just about to be "thirty years" of age. It's wonderful! It's marvelous! It will come suddenly! The Lord will do a great thing. He'll heal your mind. He'll heal your soul and heal your life. He'll turn you around. He will put your feet on a rock to stay.

I see a light! The Lord is beginning to send a light because it is about time that there be some light in your life. You have been walking in the darkness of ministry for a long time but the Lord is bringing you light. The Lord is saying that the sun is about to rise over your church.

Receive the blessing! Receive the healing! God anointed Jesus Christ with power. That power is coming into your life now! There is power to heal and save you. There is power to destroy the works of the devil. There is power to lift you higher. He is the same yesterday, today and forever.

No one who comes into contact with the anointing is ever the same again. You'll see practical changes in your life and ministry in the name of Jesus. God has turned your life around and taken you out of the miry clay of ministry. He has placed your feet upon a rock to stay. It is your season to be anointed!

CHAPTER 7

How to Recognize the Number One Manifestation of the Holy Spirit

But the Comforter, which is the Holy Ghost, whom the Father will send in my name, SHALL TEACH YOU ALL THINGS, and bring all things to your remembrance, whatsoever I have said unto you.

John 14:26

The number one manifestation of the Holy Spirit is teaching, revelation, truth, knowledge, light, insight, understanding and counsel. Jesus promised to send the Holy Spirit as our Comforter. But what is this Comforter going to do for us? How is the Holy Spirit going to comfort us? How will the Holy Spirit become visible to the average Christian?

He makes Himself visible and relevant to us by teaching us all things.

The Bible is replete with instances when the Holy Spirit became "visible" (shown, demonstrated, manifested) to believers. Amazingly, the commonest demonstration of the presence of the Spirit is the teaching! The principal job of the Holy Spirit is to teach and guide the Church. Every time you are in the presence of the teaching anointing, you must acknowledge the great presence of the Holy Spirit. He is being made visible to you. When you read your Bible and begin to have deep revelations of the Word, the Holy Spirit is being manifest.

The Presence of the Holy Spirit Is the Presence of the Teaching Anointing

Many people don't benefit from the Holy Spirit. The only way some Christians seem to have the visible presence of the Holy Spirit is by the speaking in tongues. But there is more to God and more to the Holy Spirit than speaking in tongues!

When Jesus promised the Holy Spirit, to believers, He promised us a teacher. Watch out for the teacher! Anybody who wants to get to know the Holy Spirit must experience this important way that the Holy Spirit makes Himself visible to us.

Four Effects of the Manifestation of the Teaching Anointing

1. **The manifestation of the teaching anointing gives rise to conviction.**

And when he is come, he will reprove the world of sin, and of righteousness, and of judgment:

Of sin, because they believe not on me; Of righteousness, because I go to my Father, and ye see me no more; Of judgment, because the prince of this world is judged.

John 16:8-11

The convictions that you have are there because of the Holy Spirit. When the Holy Spirit comes, He will reprove the world of sin, of righteousness and of judgment. He will also guide us into all truth. It is only when the Holy Spirit is present that people are convicted of their sins. Without the Holy Spirit's presence, the preaching would never convict anyone.

2. The manifestation of the teaching anointing gives rise to truth.

You begin to know the truth when the Holy Spirit is present. The absence of the Holy Spirit gives rise to delusions and deceptions. Through the power and presence of the Holy Spirit, you will be guided into all truth and saved from deception.

I have yet many things to say unto you, but ye cannot bear them now.

Howbeit when he, the Spirit of truth, is come, HE WILL GUIDE YOU INTO ALL TRUTH: for he shall not speak of himself; but whatsoever he shall hear, that shall he speak: and he will shew you things to come.

John 16:12-13

3. The manifestation of the teaching anointing gives rise to reminders.

The Holy Spirit will also remind us of everything that Jesus has told us in His Word.

...AND BRING ALL THINGS TO YOUR REMEMBRANCE, whatsoever I have said unto you.

John 14:26

When Jesus promised us the Holy Spirit, He was promising us someone who would remind us of certain things. The Holy Spirit must be manifested to you as a "reminder". You do not know the Holy Spirit if you do not know him as a "reminder". This is all part of the Holy Spirit's ministry of teaching us. When the Holy Spirit becomes a teacher to you, he will remind you about all things you have been taught.

4. The manifestation of the teaching anointing gives rise to knowledge.

According as his divine power HATH GIVEN UNTO US ALL THINGS THAT PERTAIN UNTO LIFE AND GODLINESS, THROUGH THE KNOWLEDGE OF HIM that hath called us to glory and virtue:

2 Peter 1:3

What are the things that pertain to life? The things that pertain to life are money, cars, clothes, houses, healing, jobs, good jobs, wives, husbands, children, health, education, long life, prosperity, peace, joy in the Holy Spirit, financial blessings, knowledge, wisdom, good pastors, friends etc. You may be asking, "How is God going to give me all things that pertain unto life?"

The Scripture says, "God hath given us all things that pertain unto life *through the knowledge of him* that has called us to glory and virtue". In other words God knows that we will receive all things that pertain unto life when we get to know Him better. That is why He sent the Comforter. He sent the Comforter to teach us and to give us knowledge. The knowledge the Holy Spirit gives us about God, will lead us into everything that pertains to this life.

You must understand that the Comforter is here to teach you. He is here to manifest Himself as a teacher in your life. That is why you must read and study your Bible!

Perhaps the strongest manifestation of the Spirit is the preaching and the teaching. Unfortunately, the teaching is usually regarded as the powerless part of the ministration. When people scream, fall and shiver we say, "Oh, the Holy Spirit is at work." But when the teaching is going on, we say to ourselves, "It is not yet time for the power." This is unfortunate, because the Holy Spirit's primary visible role is in teaching us His Word.

The Holy Spirit and Knowledge

The principal work of the Holy Spirit is to guide us into all truth. When you allow him to teach you, you will have access to everything that pertains to life and to godliness.

Then through the Word of God you will receive all things that pertain unto godliness! Churches are full of people who want miracles and breakthroughs. If you want a permanent breakthrough then you must believe the Bible because it says, "And ye shall know the truth, and the truth shall make you free," (John 8:32).

I have a revelation of Heaven. I know it is the most important place to be and I want to go there. I have a revelation of serving the Lord. That is why I want to serve Him more. I have a revelation that it is more important to get to Heaven and to serve the Lord than to do anything else. These revelations came to me through the knowledge of the Word.

Thank God for the miracles. Thank God for all the things He is going to do to make Himself visible in our lives. But He comes first and foremost as a teacher, and as someone guiding and leading.

Receive the knowledge of His Word! By His Word you can be free!

You don't have to sin, you don't have to die; you don't have to kill yourself! God is setting you free!

Don't die before your time! God is saving you; He is saving your life and extending your life through the knowledge of His Word.

You are free by the power of the Lord!

You can live a righteous life!

You can do the right thing because the Lord is your helper. He said, "I will send the Comforter, the helper, a stand-by, the strengthener."

He will strengthen you!

You will not fall by the wayside!

You will not die before your time!

He will bring you all these blessings through His Word!

Most of us have never asked the Holy Spirit to teach us personally. I constantly pray for God to give me the spirit of wisdom and revelation in the knowledge of His Word.

Churches are full of spiritual babies seeking for miracles and signs. But Jesus said it is an evil generation that looks for signs.

And when the people were gathered thick together, he began to say, This is an evil generation: they seek a sign; and there shall no sign be given it, but the sign of Jonas the prophet.

Luke 11:29

If you want a permanent blessing then you need the Holy Spirit as a teacher. If you want to walk into everything that pertains to this life and to godliness, then you need the Holy Spirit to be demonstrated as a teacher in your life.

Life is made up of two compartments, your natural life and your spiritual life. When one side is not working, it affects the other. That is why God has given us things that pertain to the natural and to the supernatural; all things that pertain unto life and godliness - through His Holy Spirit. You will not go far with God until you ask the Holy Spirit to teach you.

Rise through Knowledge

Even in the secular world it is through knowledge that you move into higher positions. Those who are educated rule those who are not educated. The greatest victories that you will ever have will come through knowledge. Those who have knowledge suppress and oppress those who do not have it. The people who know how to make things like aeroplanes, ships and cars, rule the rest of the world.

With time, countries that have more knowledge have dominated those with less knowledge. It is a fact of life. At different workplaces, those with higher education earn much more than those with lower education. What separates the two? What is the dividing line? It is knowledge. Knowledge sets you apart in this life.

It is exactly the same with spiritual things. Knowledge puts you in another category. When you know certain things, you move ahead in life and in ministry.

Don't cut off the Teacher!

You may love miracles but if you really want everything that pertains to life and godliness, welcome the Holy Spirit as a teacher! That is phanerosis.

I knew and respected Kenneth Hagin very much. At a Winter Bible Seminar in Tulsa, I was astounded as this man simply taught from the Bible everyday. Every morning and evening, it was the Word that had pre-eminence. I respected the power of the teaching anointing even more as I watched crowds gather to receive His simple teachings. I had thought that such a great man of God would come breathing fire and miracles. But all he did was to teach!

Let's get into the Holy Spirit. Let's ask Him to teach us. He will give us knowledge. You are being taught now so that you can avoid making some grievous mistakes. You must feel the presence of the Holy Spirit in every quiet time you have.

I dissected frogs, analyzed blood vessels, and did so many things when I was in medical school. How has it helped me? Of what use is the frog that I dissected? How is it helping me now? However, this Word that I read has given me wisdom and direction for my life and ministry. It is time to get the knowledge. The Holy Spirit will be made visible to you as a teacher. God is leading His people into a wonderful life through the knowledge of Him!

CHAPTER 8

What is a Manifestation of the Holy Spirit?

Now concerning spiritual gifts, brethren, I would not have you ignorant. Ye know that ye were Gentiles, carried away unto these dumb idols, even as ye were led.

Wherefore I give you to understand, that no man speaking by the Spirit of God calleth Jesus accursed: and that no man can say that Jesus is the Lord, but by the Holy Ghost.

Now there are diversities of gifts, but the same Spirit. And there are differences of administrations, but the same Lord. And there are diversities of operations, but it is the same God which worketh all in all.

But the manifestation of the Spirit is given to every man to profit withal.

1 Corinthians 12:1-7

Thank God for the greatness of the Holy Spirit in Heaven. Thank God for the wonders of the Holy Spirit in the Bible. But I need the Holy Spirit practically, tangibly and visibly today.

God knows how we need a comforter who can be contacted! He knows we need a Holy Spirit who is made visible whenever necessary. What is the use of a car you cannot see, and money you cannot touch? Thank God for all the cars in Japan and Korea but I need one that I can touch and feel. Thank God for all the money in the banks of America and Germany, but I need some in my hand now. I need money I can touch, hold and spend. Thank God for the Holy Spirit in Heaven. But I need the Holy Spirit here and now.

Notice how Paul talks about the *"manifestations of the spirit."* The word *"manifestation"* used here is the Greek word *"phanerosis"* which means, *"to make visible."*

Paul is saying in other words, that the making visible (*manifestation*) of the Holy Spirit is given for everybody's benefit. Everyone needs the Holy Spirit to be made visible from time to time. To be made visible, is to be made tangible and available. The Holy Spirit often makes Himself visible through manifestations such as shaking, trembling, convulsing, crying, screaming and falling.

Phanerosis: To Make Visible

Phanerosis, which is translated "manifestation" also means: a sign, an expression, a demonstration, the symptom, the appearance and the materialisation of an invisible thing. 1 Corinthians 12:7 therefore reads: "The sign, the expression, the demonstration, the symptom, the appearance and the materialisation of the Holy Spirit is given to everyone to profit withal."

God manifested Himself in various ways to those who believed in Him. This is something God did in the past and is still doing today. Because the Holy Spirit is alive in us, there are times when He makes Himself visible to us. Without the Holy Spirit becoming visible, we will not benefit from Him.

The phanerosis of the Holy Spirit or the making visible of the Spirit is real. Many times you can feel the presence of the Holy Spirit at meetings. When you sense the presence of the Holy Spirit, He is making Himself visible.

Sometimes I have sensed the Holy Spirit move through the auditorium. Sometimes I sense Him sweep through the balcony and sometimes He is on the stage. I have seen the Holy Spirit bring healing to people in the congregation. There are times that I can feel Him in the car with me and then I start to cry like a baby. I sometimes need to drive alone because of the Holy Spirit. When He is present, He does so many things in my life.

And when the day of Pentecost was fully come, they were all with one accord in one place. And suddenly THERE CAME A SOUND from heaven as of a rushing mighty wind, and it filled all the house where they were sitting.

Acts 2:1-2

Thank God for a tangible sound from the presence of the Holy Spirit. There is a tangible dimension of the Holy Spirit. There is a dimension in which the Holy Spirit moves out of the invisible, the intangible, to the visible, the tangible and the touchable. He is a spirit but he also operates in the physical dimension.

Sometimes, people experience the Holy Spirit at miracle services and even feel Him. They say things like, "I felt a cool breeze come over me." We are used to the love, patience, goodness and gentleness of the Spirit. We are used to people speaking in tongues. We are used to all these things. But we need to open up to the other dimension where the Holy Spirit does things in the tangible and physical dimension.

It is in this dimension that you begin to see healings taking place. That is when the invisible becomes visible and physical changes happen. Would there not be some sound if somebody walked into a room? That is why they heard the sound of wind when the Holy Spirit descended on the day of Pentecost. They saw tongues of fire and they heard the sound of wind. The invisible had now become visible. The untouchable had now become tangible.

Everyone must benefit from the manifestation of the Holy Spirit. He is given for our benefit.

I have seen the manifestations of the Holy Spirit. This is what has transformed our church from a classroom church to a congregation in a cathedral. The Holy Spirit is the rain. Things grow when there is rain! Plants flourish in the rain! The rain of the Holy Spirit is what will bring transformation to the ministry. The Holy Spirit will make Himself visible by transforming your little Bible study group into a worldwide ministry.

It is very important for us to have the power of God in our midst because when there is no power in the church, the members wander off into the occult world looking for help. Often, when people are in crisis and need spiritual help, they do not turn to the church but to the devil.

People don't see power in the churches they belong to. That is why they go seeking for help elsewhere.

We need to have the power of God in the church to cater for the needs of people. We must experience manifestations of the Holy Spirit at our meetings.

I remember experiencing the power of the Holy Spirit when a visiting minister came to my church. After he had finished ministering, he called my wife and I to pray for us. As he laid his hands on me, I felt the manifestation of the Holy Spirit. It felt like waves of oil were coming down over me. I had never felt anything like that before. I experienced Phanerosis – the making visible of the Holy Spirit. I knew that the Lord was anointing me.

If you have never experienced the Holy Spirit in a visible way, it is not because He is not real. It is because He has never been made visible in your life.

From today, *phanerosis* is going to happen in your life in the name of Jesus! You will see Him moving practically in your life!

CHAPTER 9

Seeing and Knowing in the Ministry of Jesus

For to one is given by the Spirit the word of wisdom; to another the word of knowledge by the same Spirit;

To another faith by the same Spirit; to another the gifts of healing by the same Spirit;

To another the working of miracles; to another prophecy; to another discerning of spirits; to another divers kinds of tongues; to another the interpretation of tongues:

1 Corinthians 12:8-10

Elisha's servant's eyes were opened to see the spiritual armies around him.Seeing and knowing involves two major manifestations of the Spirit. These two manifestations are the most awesome ways in which the Holy Spirit makes Himself visible. Another name for the combined gifts of the word of knowledge and the discerning of spirits, is "seeing and knowing." Every minister must pray for the grace of seeing and knowing. As Shakespeare said, "There is no art to find the mind's construction in the face." This means that you can hardly know the thoughts and intentions of men by looking in their faces.

Seeing and knowing things supernaturally, is a gift that can operate in your life. One of the most famous examples of seeing and knowing is when Elisha prayed that his servant would see the mountain full of horses and chariots. "And Elisha prayed, and said, LORD, I pray thee, open his eyes, that he may see. And the LORD opened the eyes of the young man; and he saw: and, behold, the mountain was full of horses and chariots of fire round about Elisha" (2 Kings 6:17).

When the Holy Spirit manifests *a word of knowledge* to you, you will begin to know things supernaturally. You must pray for the supernatural ability of seeing and knowing things! A minister must know things in a supernatural way.

The manifestation of seeing and knowing involves seeing and detecting evil spirits. To be able to discern or distinguish the presence of evil spirits you must have the Holy Spirit. The spirit realm is where God lives. That is the realm where demons and angels operate. When you have the manifestation of seeing and knowing, you will see and detect angels, demons and the Spirit of God. Jesus constantly operated in the gift of seeing and knowing.

Seven Times That Jesus Operated in the Gift of Seeing and Knowing

1. **Jesus knew how many men the woman of Samaria had slept with.**

    Jesus saith unto her, Go, call thy husband, and come hither. The woman answered and said, I have no husband. Jesus said unto her, Thou hast well said, I have no husband:

    For thou hast had five husbands; and he whom thou now hast is not thy husband: in that saidst thou truly.

    John 4:16-18

2. **Jesus saw and talked to the two dead prophets Elijah and Moses on the mount.**

    And was transfigured before them: and his face did shine as the sun, and his raiment was white as the light. And, behold, there appeared unto them Moses and Elias talking with him.

    Matthew 17:2-3

3. **Jesus saw and detected angels in the Garden of Gethsemane.**

    And he was withdrawn from them about a stone's cast, and kneeled down, and prayed, Saying, Father, if thou be willing, remove this cup from me: nevertheless not my will, but thine, be done. And there appeared an angel unto him from heaven, strengthening him.

    Luke 22:41-43

    Jesus knew the people who did not believe in Him. There are three groups of negative people that Jesus was aware of.

4. **Jesus knew when people were murmuring against Him.**

    When Jesus knew in himself that his disciples murmured at it, he said unto them, Doth this offend you?

    John 6:61

5. Jesus knew the people who did not believe in Him.

But there are some of you that believe not. For Jesus knew from the beginning who they were that believed not, and who should betray him.

John 6:64

6. Jesus knew the people who would betray Him.

But there are some of you that believe not. For Jesus knew from the beginning who they were that believed not, and who should betray him.

John 6:64

7. Jesus knew which of His disciples was demon-possessed.

Jesus answered them, Have not I chosen you twelve, and one of you is a devil? He spake of Judas Iscariot the son of Simon: for he it was that should betray him, being one of the twelve.

John 6:70-71

There are many times I have known people who did not believe in me. They would sit in a group and all seem to be eagerly in the flow. But I knew that this one did not believe in me.

I remember one occasion when I said to my associate pastor, "Do you see this fellow?"

He said, "Yes, I do."

Then I told him, "One day he will leave us and betray us."

At that time, there was no sign of any such possibility.

Two years later, what I said came to pass exactly as I had predicted. This fellow left us and spoke bitterly against me. You see, God had shown it to me by the gift of *seeing and knowing*. I was prepared for it because God had shown it to me.

I remember one pastor who was totally devastated by the betrayal of one of his dearest friends and associates. We sat together at a dinner table as he recounted his experiences.

He told me, "Whenever this pastor travelled abroad, he would bring me nice gifts."

He continued, "Sometimes he would buy me a neck tie. At other times, he would present me with an envelope containing some dollars or pounds sterling."

He lamented, "I thought he loved me, I thought he was with me, I thought these gifts meant something"

Dear friend, don't forget that Jesus enjoyed dinner with someone who hated him. On the outward, they all looked happy and committed but Jesus knew what He needed to know.

May you have the gift of *seeing and knowing* manifesting in your life when you need it!

CHAPTER 10

How to Operate in the Manifestation of Seeing and Knowing

For to one is given by the Spirit the word of wisdom; to another the word of knowledge by the same Spirit; To another faith by the same Spirit; to another the gifts of healing by the same Spirit; To another the working of miracles; to another prophecy; to another discerning of spirits; to another divers kinds of tongues; to another the interpretation of tongues:

1 Corinthians 12:8-10

1. The manifestation of seeing and knowing is for your protection.

One day, I came to church two hours before time and noticed one young lady who was sitting at the back and praying. I couldn't help noticing how spiritual this lady seemed to be. She would come to church earlier than everybody else. She would sit alone at the back and intercede for hours. Her prayers were not the feeble whispering kind. They were manly, strong, fervent and intense. She spoke in the tongues of angels and she prayed in the spirit.

On many different occasions I would come to church early and find only this lady interceding intensely at the back. There were times I wondered who was more spiritual: myself or this lady? I asked myself, "Who is the leader, myself or this lady?" I never said a word to her nor asked her any questions. I wouldn't want to disturb such a prayerful person.

One day, the Lord said to me, "Cause her to know her abominations."

I said, "What!"

The Lord said, "That girl is a bad girl; cause her to know her abominations,"

I said, "That is not possible. This is the most spiritual member of my church. I am even intimidated by her prayers."

I told the Lord, "She is the only one who comes early to pray. " But after a while, I felt convicted to obey the Lord. Sometimes, there are thoughts that do not go away. They seem to linger around in your spirit till you attend to them.

In the end, I sat down with this spiritual sister and said, "The Lord says I should let you know your abominations." I was sure that I was wrong about what I was saying.

As I spoke, she looked at me in amazement and began to cry. This lady then told me about her life. She told me that every time she travelled outside the country, she slept with somebody different. She went on to explain to me how she had slept with more than two hundred different people as a young person. She confessed that she was a serial and regular fornicator in spite of her super spiritual presentation.

The gift of seeing and knowing was in manifestation! God gave me the grace to see and to know. Perhaps, it was given to protect me. I needed to know the kind of person who was praying at the back of the church. Perhaps, I would have considered getting closer to her because she was so spiritual. The gift of seeing and knowing is for your protection.

2. The manifestation of seeing and knowing is to give you direction.

One night, I was in my room praying. It was a Saturday night and I was preparing to preach the next day. The Spirit of the Lord came upon me. I could not move as the Spirit spoke to me. I was alert and fixed in my chair.

The Spirit of the Lord spoke to me almost audibly about a rebellious person in the church. He revealed how this person was pretending to be faithful when in fact he was full of rebellion. I was *seeing and knowing*! Then He asked me to do certain things in church on Sunday that would expose the hypocrisy of this pastor. He said to me, "Blow the trumpet with clarity, give a clear command to the troops and you will see what will happen."

The Holy Spirit told me what would happen if I followed His instruction. The next day, I followed the Spirit's instructions to the letter. Amazingly, this rebellious fellow did exactly what the Spirit said he would do and he was exposed.

Within minutes, everything was out in the open and the solution to a long-standing problem had come.

3. The manifestation of seeing and knowing is to deliver you from the liars around you.

Leaders are often lied to. There is often no way to tell whether someone is telling the truth or not. The deceptions of a leader can lead to his downfall. Many leaders depend on what their advisers and informants tell them. When they are fed with untruths, they often make grievous mistakes that lead to corruption and embarrassment. Many political leaders come out of office, only to discover that they were deceived whilst they were in office. They were fed with lies by sycophants and bottom-licking subordinates.

One day, the Holy Spirit manifested through the gift of seeing and knowing. He revealed to me that a particular pastor had been lying to me about many different things. I became fixated in my bed, as the Holy Spirit said, "He is a liar and I will show you five different things that he has lied to you about since you have known him." Then suddenly He revealed a string of unrelated lies that this fellow had told me. Some of these lies dated back several years.

I was astounded. I had never known that all those things were lies. This revelation came so quickly that immediately after the revelation, I could not remember it anymore. God wanted to show me that the revelation did not come from my mind and that is why I could not remember it afterward. It took time and prayer to bring back the revelation. Later on, all these issues were proven to be lies.

Through the gift of *seeing and knowing*, I was able to uncover the liar within and eventually root him out of the system.

4. **The manifestation of seeing and knowing is to expose disloyalty.**

   Alexander the coppersmith did me much evil: the Lord reward him according to his works: Of whom be thou ware also; for he hath greatly withstood our words.
   2 Timothy 4:14-15

I love to have good anointed music in my services. Anointed music greatly influences the atmosphere and causes miracles to take place.

Years ago, I had a lady who used to sing beautifully in our church. She would sing a solo for me every Sunday. One night, I had a dream. Dreaming is part of seeing and knowing. In the dream, I was in a boxing ring and to my surprise; I was one of the boxers in the ring. I was wearing boxing gloves and so was my opponent. But the even greater surprise was my opponent. Believe it or not, my opponent was this lady singer!

The boxing bout began and the lady fought against me with all her might. I fought back and suddenly the dream ended.

The Lord had supernaturally revealed to me that this lady was fighting against me spiritually. Later on, I found out that she was one of the people who criticized me greatly and fought against me with her words. God delivered me from the power of this disloyal person through the gift of seeing and knowing.

5. The manifestation of seeing and knowing is to give you victory over the enemy.

Visions are also manifestations of the Holy Spirit. Visions are an advanced type of *seeing and knowing*. There have been times when the Lord opened my eyes to see visions. There was a time when I experienced a strong attack of the devil. The pressure and the deception were so strong that I was at breaking point.

One night, while on a journey, I had a vision of Satan. I was awakened at about three a.m. I suddenly saw a tall black being standing to the right of my bed. This being began to laugh and mock at me. Then I noticed that the face of this being was the face of someone I had known some years ago. This particular individual had mocked me in the past and had said certain things to despise me. It was the spirit of a mocker and the spirit of confusion. The Lord showed me the kind of spirit that was harassing my life. Confusion is one of the top strategies of Satan against ministers.

Immediately, I jumped out of my bed. There was no one in the apartment where I was living and I was all alone. I was confused and wondered what had happened. I knew that I had seen the devil at close range and that a great evil was determined against me. I felt as though I was all alone in a haunted house. I decided to have communion by myself.

I will never forget that midnight communion because I believe it ministered healing to me and also ministered the power of the blood on my life. The blood gave me victory over the devil and all his plans. Through this vision, the Lord had shown me who and what was fighting against me. The result of this vision was the termination of a particular battle that I had been fighting.

6. The manifestation of seeing and knowing is to deliver you from evil.

One day, I became ill and needed to take some medication. However at that time of my life, I believed that it was not necessary to take medicine if you had faith. Since I was endeavouring to be a real man of faith, I had decided to go on without taking any medication at all. On this particular occasion, I had decided that I would either be healed without medicine or die.

As the days went by, I became more and more ill until I was confined to my room. My family did not know what was happening to me because they thought I was just resting in my room. I was determined to rise and be healed without medicine or die by faith. As time went by, I became fixed to my bed, unable to do anything. I was waiting for God to heal me.

I believe the Lord knew how determined I was to be healed without medicine or die. By this time, the only thing I could do was to turn around in bed. At one point, I turned my head to the right and there on my bedside table was an imp-like creature. I knew at once that I was looking at an evil spirit. I knew that I was in danger even though I did not understand what I could be doing wrong. I suddenly felt that I had to take medicine to avoid the devil destroying me. I arose from the bed and took medicine at once. Through the manifestation of seeing and knowing, I was delivered from death.

7. The manifestation of seeing and knowing is to detect the presence of angels.

Several years ago, I got lost in a train station in Europe. Not only was I lost, but I was also greatly behind schedule and about to miss an all-important connection. Suddenly, a man whom I didn't know offered to help me. Strangely, the man took me from where I was through many winding corridors, staircases and tunnels to the exact spot that I needed to get to. This strange white man said he was not going where I was going but spent fifteen to twenty minutes taking me to where I needed to be.

If you know anything about Europe, you will know that this is "strange" behaviour. As strangely as he appeared, this man disappeared from the platform. I remember this incident even though it has been many years since it happened. I believe that man was an angel.

Be not forgetful to entertain strangers: for thereby some have entertained angels unawares.

Hebrews 13:2

One day, while sitting on a plane, I had a vision of an angel. He was sitting on my left-hand side wearing a light blue gown. He seemed to be relaxed but on duty. I knew I was seeing an angel on guard and I was comforted on the flight.

The Lord opened the eyes of a young lady in the congregation. As I was ministering, I would speak out blessings and words of faith. Her eyes were opened and she saw a large angel standing on my left-hand side.

As I spoke the blessings, this large angel would throw out parcels into the congregation. Many people whose arms were outstretched would receive the parcels. There were smaller angels who would take the parcels from the big angel and give it to the people in the congregation. Angels are real and they accompany us and assist us while we minister.

I remember a testimony of someone whose eyes were opened as a man of God ministered. As the man of God was preaching the person saw an angel walking around him. From time to time the angel would whisper certain things in the ears of the man of God and he would smile, nod and continue preaching. The minister himself was not aware of the presence of the angels. Is it not encouraging to know that angels are walking around you as you minister?

I was in a Kenneth Hagin service one night when an angel appeared to him. The angel asked him to follow him. Kenneth Hagin followed the angel down the aisle. When the angel got to a particular man, the angel motioned to him to minister to that particular person.

Papa Hagin then told us how the angel had directed him to minister to a particular person. The atmosphere in the meeting was absolutely charged and the service was electrifying!

It is real. The manifestations happen to every man to profit withal. We all benefit from the manifestations of the Spirit. It makes a lot of difference to us when we know what is happening in the spirit realm.

8. The manifestation of seeing and knowing is to see Jesus Christ Himself.

And I turned to see the voice that spake with me. And being turned, I saw seven golden candlesticks; And in the midst of the seven candlesticks one like unto the Son of man, clothed with a garment down to the foot, and girt about the paps with a golden girdle.

Revelation 1:12-13

Once, I was praying for eight people at a miracle service. The Lord opened the eyes of someone in the meeting and the person saw the Lord Jesus walking behind me. Suddenly, she saw the Lord Jesus move into me and then I was no longer there. She could not see me. She could only see the Lord Jesus laying hands on the people.

One of the people I was praying for testified that she felt an extreme and unusual love when hands were laid on her. This love was Jesus' love for her as he laid hands on her. Amazingly, this lady was later declared healed of cancer.

These are wonderful visions of Jesus that bring encouragement. Once, I met an elderly American lady who said to me, "I saw the Lord walking behind you when you were ministering."

She told me, "I have very real visions."

She continued, "Tonight I saw a rare and unusual phenomenon of the Lord Himself walking behind you as you were ministering. " Then she asked me, "Do you know that the Lord walks behind you in that way when you minister?"

I smiled and told her I didn't know that.

On another occasion, I was ministering at a little camp meeting in a foreign country. As I laid hands on the people, the Lord opened the eyes of one of our sisters. She was amazed at what she saw. The Lord Jesus was sitting on one of the chairs behind the pulpit. He was observing what I was doing. She was greatly touched by this vision and gave glory to God.

CHAPTER 11

The New Testament List of Manifestations

For to one is given by the Spirit the word of wisdom; to another the word of knowledge by the same Spirit; To another faith by the same Spirit; to another the gifts of healing by the same Spirit;

To another the working of miracles; to another prophecy; to another discerning of spirits; to another divers kinds of tongues; to another the interpretation of tongues:

1 Corinthians 12:8-10

This Scripture gives us a list of manifestations of the Spirit. However, there are many other assorted manifestations that are not in this list. They are found scattered throughout the Bible. Whether the manifestations are in the Corinthians list or not does not matter. What matters is that they are manifestations of the Holy Spirit.

1. The Word of Wisdom

The word of wisdom gives you the wisdom to know how to handle complex situations. Wisdom is profitable to direct.

2. The Gift of Faith

This is supernatural faith to speak and to do things that God has called you to. The gift of faith operated in Isaac when he blessed his two sons, Jacob and Esau.

> **And his father Isaac said unto him, Come near now, and kiss me, my son. And he came near, and kissed him: and he smelled the smell of his raiment, and blessed him, and said, See, the smell of my son is as the smell of a field which the LORD hath blessed:**
>
> **Therefore God give thee of the dew of heaven, and the fatness of the earth, and plenty of corn and wine:**
>
> **Let people serve thee, and nations bow down to thee: be Lord over thy brethren, and let thy mother's sons bow down to thee: cursed be every one that curseth thee, and blessed be he that blesseth thee.**
>
> **Genesis 27:26-29**

Up until today, this blessing persists in the life of Israel. It is as though God Himself had spoken these blessings even though it was a man speaking. Watch out for when the Holy Spirit comes on people who speak to you prophetically. That is the manifestation of the gift of faith.

The same manifestation operated in Jacob, when he blessed and cursed his children.

And Jacob called unto his sons, and said, Gather yourselves together, that I may tell you that which shall befall you in the last days. Gather yourselves together, and hear, ye sons of Jacob; and hearken unto Israel your father.

Reuben, thou art my firstborn, my might, and the beginning of my strength, the excellency of dignity, and the excellency of power:

Unstable as water, thou shalt not excel; because thou wentest up to thy father's bed; then defiledst thou it: he went up to my couch. Simeon and Levi are brethren; instruments of cruelty are in their habitations.

Genesis 49:1-5

3. The Working of Miracles

The working of miracles is the manifestation of non-healing miracles. Jesus did several non-healing miracles. In a sense, these miracles are more astonishing than the healings. The book of John contains some of these non-healing miracles.

The Working of Miracles in the Ministry of Jesus

a. The changing of water into wine

Jesus saith unto them, Fill the waterpots with water. And they filled them up to the brim. And he saith unto them, Draw out now, and bear unto the governor of the feast. And they bare it. When the ruler of the feast had tasted the water that was made wine, and knew not whence it was: (but the servants which drew the water knew;) the governor of the feast called the bridegroom,

This beginning of miracles did Jesus in Cana of Galilee, and manifested forth his glory; and his disciples believed on him.

John 2:7-9, 11

b. The multiplying of the bread and fish

And Jesus took the loaves; and when he had given thanks, he distributed to the disciples, and the disciples to them that were set down; and likewise of the fishes as much as they would.

When they were filled, he said unto his disciples, Gather up the fragments that remain, that nothing be lost.

Therefore they gathered them together, and filled twelve baskets with the fragments of the five barley loaves, which remained over and above unto them that had eaten. Then those men, when they had seen the miracle that Jesus did, said, This is of a truth that prophet that should come into the world.

John 6:11-14

c. Walking on the Sea of Galilee

So when they had rowed about five and twenty or thirty furlongs, they see Jesus walking on the sea, and drawing nigh unto the ship: and they were afraid. But he saith unto them, It is I; be not afraid.

John 6:19-20

4. The Gift of Healing

Jesus Christ is a healing Jesus. If the Holy Spirit is present, He can make Himself manifest by healing someone. It happened to the woman with the issue of blood in the Bible and it will happen to you in Jesus' name! Healing is a manifestation of the presence of the Holy Spirit.

In the presence of the Holy Spirit the testes can be healed.

I remember what happened at a miracle service in South Africa. There was a lady in the meeting whose child didn't have one testicle. The child was scheduled for an operation in a few weeks. She came forward in the healing line and I prayed for her child as I did for all the others. To her amazement, the testes appeared when she checked her child. The testes were right there. That is a miracle from God.

In the presence of the Holy Spirit ears can be healed.

There was a young man who had a hearing impairment in the right ear. He claimed that he could not hear if somebody spoke to him on that side of his ear. But when he was prayed for, the Spirit of God came powerfully upon him and then he realized that he could hear clearly. We demonstrated it right there in church. He could hear clearly from afar.

In the presence of the Holy Spirit knees can be healed.

There was a lady who had a knee ailment from childhood such that if she ran for a short distance, her knees would buckle and she would fall down. This happened to her once when she was crossing the road and she was almost hit by a car.

She felt a sense of heaviness in that knee and then she realised that she had been healed. She demonstrated her healing by running around the church. There was no noise and no pain in her knees. Her knee did not buckle and she was healed miraculously.

In the presence of the Holy Spirit gynaecological problems can be healed.

There was a lady who sat upstairs during one of our miracle services. She had not had her menstrual period for one year even though she was not pregnant. She just felt the power of God come over her and started bleeding in the service. She came back to testify about her healing.

I remember another lady who had been bleeding continuously for three months. The bleeding stopped right in the service. Just like the woman healed with the issue of blood under Jesus' ministry, this lady experienced a healing of an issue of blood.

This is what it is like when the Holy Spirit is manifesting Himself in healings. The Holy Spirit is there to heal you and He is there to prolong your life upon the surface of the Earth. The manifestations of healing are real today.

5. Prophecy

Prophecies are words that are spoken under the inspiration of the Holy Spirit. Prophecy is used to direct, help, influence and lead us.

There are two types of New Testament prophecy: the simple gift of prophecy and predictive prophecy. The purpose of simple prophecy is outlined in 1 Corinthians 14:3. It is for exhortation, edification and encouragement.

But he that prophesieth speaketh unto men to edification, and exhortation, and comfort.
1 Corinthians 14:3

The other type of prophecy is called predictive prophecy. In this type of prophecy, events are foretold by the prophet. The twenty-fourth chapter of Matthew is a compilation of several predictive prophecies that Christ made about this world.

And as he sat upon the mount of Olives, the disciples came unto him privately, saying, Tell us, when shall these things be? and what shall be the sign of thy coming, and of the end of the world?
Matthew 24:3

6. Divers Kinds of Tongues

The gift of tongues is the commonest manifestation of the Holy Spirit. It is a wonderful gift because it is a language from the Lord. These tongues are heavenly languages of angels. Sometimes, the tongues are human languages unknown to the speaker who is manifesting the gift. We speak in the tongues of men and of angels.

> **Though I speak with the TONGUES OF MEN AND OF ANGELS, and have not charity, I am become as sounding brass, or a tinkling cymbal.**
>
> **1 Corinthians 13:1**

> **For he that speaketh in an unknown tongue speaketh not unto men, but unto God: for no man understandeth him; howbeit in the spirit he speaketh mysteries.**
>
> **1 Corinthians 14:2**

You need to speak in tongues because there are many prayers nobody should hear. There are prayers the devil should not understand. He should not know when you command angels to kick him. When you pray in tongues, it worries the devil, because he does not know what you are saying.

Once, a pastor who had lived in Norway before, heard me speaking in tongues. As I ministered in tongues, he could hear that I was speaking pure Norgsk (the Norwegian language). The first time it happened, he was not sure whether he was hearing right. On the way home, he told his wife about it in the car. The next day, the meetings continued and he said he heard me speak pure Norgsk again. This time round he was sure about it and he came to testify. I have never been to Norway and I don't speak Norgsk. That was a powerful manifestation of the presence of the Holy Spirit. That is *phanerosis* right there!

When the Holy Spirit demonstrates His presence in this way, the Lord is giving us a glimpse of glory. He is real!

7. Interpretation of Tongues

Interpretation greatly multiplies the blessing that you get from speaking in tongues alone.

This involves speaking forth the meanings of the tongues that have been spoken. It is not the gift of translation and is therefore not a "word for word" exposé. Interpretation is a gift for everyone who speaks in tongues. Everyone who speaks in tongues must believe in and practise interpreting tongues.

Wherefore let him that speaketh in an unknown tongue pray that he may interpret. For if I pray in an unknown tongue, my spirit prayeth, but my understanding is unfruitful.

1 Corinthians 14:13-14

CHAPTER 12

The Manifestation of Falling under the Power

W e are to covet the best gifts. When you desire the manifestations of the Spirit you will have them. God is not going to give you something that you don't desire. How can you believe in healing when you don't hear about it?

> **How then shall they call on him in whom they have not believed? And how shall they believe in him of whom they have not heard? And how shall they hear without a preacher?**
>
> **Romans 10:14**

> **So then faith cometh by hearing, and hearing by the word of God.**
>
> **Romans 10:17**

As we preach about the manifestations of the Holy Spirit you develop an interest in them. You begin to desire them. As your desire grows, they begin to manifest. I realize where the people have not been taught, they don't have many miracles.

It is going to happen to you because you desire it. God is not going to give you something you don't desire. God is not going to give you something you don't even think about.

There are other demonstrations of the presence of the Holy Spirit apart from the listed manifestations in 1 Corinthians 12. These are not bunched together in one list and I call them "the unlisted manifestations of the Holy Spirit".

Why People Fall under the Power

One of the commonest unlisted manifestations of the spirit and power of God is falling down. Falling down is often caused by the wine, the wind and the rain.

1. The Wine of the Spirit

The new wine is often seen as a type of the Holy Spirit. In the natural, over-indulging in wine can lead to falling, shaking and trembling. Similarly, indulging in the wine of the Spirit can lead to falling, shaking and trembling!

For these are not drunken, as ye suppose, seeing it is but the third hour of the day. But this is that which was spoken by the prophet Joel; And it shall come to pass in the last days, saith God, I will pour out of my Spirit upon all flesh...

Acts 2:15-17

And be not drunk with wine, wherein is excess; but be filled with the Spirit;

Ephesians 5:18

2. The Wind of the Spirit

The wind bloweth where it listeth, and thou hearest the sound thereof, but canst not tell whence it cometh, and whither it goeth: so is every one that is born of the Spirit.

John 3:8

The wind is known to pull down trees and even houses. The wind of the Spirit does the same. It is time to believe that these things are real. Do you remember when Jesus breathed on His disciples and said, "Receive ye the Holy Spirit?"

And when he had said this, he breathed on them, and saith unto them, Receive ye the Holy Ghost:

John 20:22

Do you remember when the Holy Spirit came into the upper room as a mighty rushing wind? The Holy Spirit operates like a wind. Recently, at one of our miracle services, I was laying hands on all of the people who had come to the altar. One of my pastors later testified. He said, "As you approached me, a wind began to blow on me. It was a supernatural wind." He marvelled, "The Holy Spirit is so real."

3. The Rain of the Spirit

Rain is known to pull down trees and houses as well. Many people run from approaching rainstorms. God says He will come to us in the form of rain.

Then shall we know, if we follow on to know the LORD: his going forth is prepared as the morning; and he shall come unto us as the rain, as the latter and former rain unto the earth.

Hosea 6:3

Eight Examples of Falling under the Power

All through the Bible, we see people falling under the power of God.

1. The falling of the priests at the dedication of the temple

It came even to pass, as the trumpeters and singers were as one, to make one sound to be heard in praising and thanking the LORD; and when they lifted up their voice with the trumpets and cymbals and instruments of musick, and praised the LORD, saying,

For he is good; for his mercy endureth for ever: that then the house was filled with a cloud, even the house of the LORD; SO THAT THE PRIESTS COULD NOT STAND

TO MINISTER BY REASON OF THE CLOUD: for the glory of the LORD had filled the house of God.

2 Chronicles 5:13-14

The glory of the Lord at one time filled the temple so much so that the priests, the trumpeters and the musicians couldn't stand anymore. They all went down because of the glory of the Lord. These things happen. They are real.

The glory of God can be manifested at different levels. It can come over you to a point where you cannot stand. You must pray to experience the power of God so much so that you cannot stand. I want to experience the glory of God.

You should desire to get to the place where these people did. When they were worshipping, the cloud of glory filled the place so much so that the trumpeters and the priests could not stand. It was not that they did not want to stand. They could not stand!

2. The falling of the soldiers who arrested Jesus

Judas then, having received a band of men and officers from the chief priests and Pharisees, cometh thither with lanterns and torches and weapons.

Jesus therefore, knowing all things that should come upon him, went forth, and said unto them, Whom seek ye? They answered him, Jesus of Nazareth. Jesus saith unto them, I am he.

And Judas also, which betrayed him, stood with them. As soon then as he had said unto them, I AM HE, THEY WENT BACKWARD, AND FELL TO THE GROUND.

John 18:3-6

What happened as soon as Jesus said "I am He?" The attackers went backward and fell to the ground. Everybody fell under the anointing. There was no usher to support them. There was nothing to protect them as they went backwards and fell down. Wow! You realize right there that the Holy Spirit was in action. That alone should have frightened the soldiers away.

3. The falling of the Apostle Paul's entourage on the road to Damascus

Why should it be thought a thing incredible with you, that God should raise the dead?

I verily thought with myself, that I ought to do many things contrary to the name of Jesus of Nazareth. Which thing I also did in Jerusalem: and many of the saints did I shut up in prison, having received authority from the chief priests; and when they were put to death, I gave my voice against them.

And I punished them oft in every synagogue, and compelled them to blaspheme; and being exceedingly mad against them, I persecuted them even unto strange cities.

Whereupon as I went to Damascus with authority and commission from the chief priests, At midday, O king, I saw in the way a light from heaven, above the brightness of the sun, shining round about me and them which journeyed with me.

AND WHEN WE WERE ALL FALLEN TO THE EARTH, I heard a voice speaking unto me, and saying in the Hebrew tongue, Saul, Saul, why persecutest thou me? it is hard for thee to kick against the pricks.

Acts 26:8-14

Paul described how he and his companions fell under the power on the road to Damascus. When Paul's companions saw the light around them, they all fell to the ground. That was a manifestation of the Holy Spirit. When people fall under the power, everybody wonders if it is real. No matter how many times people see it happen they still watch and wonder. Sometimes you can see from the way people fall under the power that something unusual has happened to them. Some kind of power has struck them! I keep wondering about it myself even though I see it happen over and over again.

I remember I was speaking to a lady whom I had prayed for. Later, she told me what had happened to her when I was ministering to her. She described how she had fallen down during the ministration.

I asked her, "Do you normally fall under the power?"

She said, "I never fall, I am not the falling kind." She thought that there were some types of people who were prone to fall under the power.

She continued, "I never fall, I don't fall. But this time I fell and I fell again and again. I fell so many times and I did not know what was happening to me. I was completely powerless to control myself and stand on my feet. I simply could not stand when you touched me."

It is indeed a wonder. Falling under the power will make you wonder what is going on. Falling under the power is a sign and a wonder. People who fall under the power are not necessarily healed. When people fall, they may be healed or not healed. They just fall. It is a sign and it is a wonder! It is a manifestation of the Holy Spirit.

4. Balaam's ass fell at the sight of the angel of the Lord

And when the ass saw the angel of the Lord, she fell down under Balaam: and Balaam's anger was kindled, and he smote the ass with a staff.

Numbers 22:27

The falling of Balaam's ass at the sight of the angel refutes allegations that when people fall under the power they are psychologically induced to do so. How could the donkey have been psychologically manipulated to fall down at a particular time? When the donkey came into contact with the spirit realm, he simply fell down. This is what happens to many people. They are not manipulated or psychologically caused to fall down! They just have a spiritual experience that makes them fall down.

5. Eli fell at the mention of the ark of the Lord

And it came to pass, when he made mention of the ark of God, that HE FELL FROM OFF THE SEAT backward by the side of the gate, and his neck brake, and he died: for

he was an old man, and heavy. And he had judged Israel
forty years.

1 Samuel 4:18

This experience of falling down also does refute the allegation
that if people are made to fall down by the Holy Spirit, they will
not hurt themselves. Some people would say that if the power
of the Holy Spirit makes someone fall down, the person should
come to no harm. However, we have seen numerous cases of
people falling under the power and getting hurt.

This is nothing new and Eli even died after falling under the
power and breaking his neck. It is important to have good ushers
to prevent people from getting hurt when they fall under the
power.

6.   Ezekiel fell at the sight of the glory of the Lord

As the appearance of the bow that is in the cloud in the
day of rain, so was the appearance of the brightness round
about. This was the appearance of the likeness of the glory
of the LORD.
And WHEN I SAW IT, I FELL upon my face, and I heard
a voice of one that spake.

Ezekiel 1:28

7.   The Apostle John fell at the sight of the Lord

And WHEN I SAW HIM, I FELL at his feet as dead. And
he laid his right hand upon me, saying unto me, Fear not; I
am the first and the last:

Revelation 1:17

To "fall as dead" means that Apostle John dropped to the
ground suddenly. To "fall as dead" is not a composed and
dignified fall. To "fall as dead" means to collapse uncontrollably
to the ground. When the power of God is moving, you will see
many people fall to the ground as though they are dead.

8. Daniel fell as God spoke to him

So he came near where I stood: and WHEN HE CAME,
I WAS AFRAID, AND FELL upon my face: but he said
unto me, Understand, O son of man: for at the time of the
end shall be the vision.

Daniel 8:17

Daniel also fell under the power when he came in contact with
spiritual things. Daniel was a prime minister and he was highly
placed in society. But he fell under the power when he came in
contact with spiritual realities.

Dear friend, there is enough evidence in the Word of God for
you to accept these manifestations of the Spirit. Ministers must
flow in the reality of God's power. Understand the Word of God
and you will experience the richness in all that God has for us.

CHAPTER 13

Powerful Assorted Manifestations

1. Weeping and Crying

And Elisha came to Damascus; and Ben-hadad the king of Syria was sick; and it was told him, saying, The man of God is come hither. And the king said unto Hazael, Take a present in thine hand, and go, meet the man of God, and inquire of the LORD by him, saying, Shall I recover of this disease?

So Hazael went to meet him, and took a present with him, even of every good thing of Damascus, forty camels' burden, and came and stood before him, and said, Thy son Ben-hadad king of Syria hath sent me to thee, saying, Shall I recover of this disease?

And Elisha said unto him, Go, say unto him, Thou mayest certainly recover: howbeit the LORD hath shewed me that he shall surely die. And he settled his countenance stedfastly, until he was ashamed: AND THE MAN OF GOD WEPT.

And Hazael said, WHY WEEPETH MY LORD? And he answered, Because I know the evil that thou wilt do unto the children of Israel: their strong holds wilt thou set on fire, and their young men wilt thou slay with the sword, and wilt dash their children, and rip up their women with child. And Hazael said, But what, is thy servant a dog, that he should do this great thing?

And Elisha answered, The LORD hath shewed me that thou shalt be king over Syria.

So he departed from Elisha, and came to his master; who said to him, What said Elisha to thee? And he answered, He told me that thou shouldest surely recover.

And it came to pass on the morrow, that he took a thick cloth, and dipped it in water, and spread it on his face, so that he died: and Hazael reigned in his stead.

2 Kings 8:7-15

Weeping and crying are some of the commonest manifestations of the Holy Spirit. They are manifestations that come when the anointing of the Lord comes on people. Crying is one of the deepest human emotions. It is not easy to fake crying and weeping. They are usually involuntary expressions and reactions to something. I have tried to make myself cry. I once wanted to cry while I preached because I realised it had a powerful effect on the listeners. I tried and tried but never succeeded even once in bringing out any tears.

I have noticed how people begin to weep when the Spirit ministers to them. I notice, commonly, how many people start crying when I lay hands on them. There were times when I myself would start weeping when I laid hands on certain people. I have often wondered why this happened. I think the answer is in the text above.

When the Spirit ministers to a person, the Lord shows and reveals certain things to the person that touch the deepest emotions within. The person starts weeping uncontrollably because of what he sees or realises so clearly.

Under the anointing, Elisha stared at Hazael until he was embarrassed. Elisha then began to cry. Hazael asked Elisha why he was crying and Elisha simply told him what he was seeing. As Elisha looked at Hazael, he saw a horrendous murderer who would unleash a reign of terror on the people of Israel. The realisation of how brutal and murderous this man standing before him would be, touched the deepest part of Elisha's heart and he began to cry. "**...and the man of God wept. And Hazael said, Why weepeth my lord? And he answered, Because I know the evil that thou wilt do unto the children of Israel.**"

Elisha then described the details of the terrible deeds this man would do in the future. He saw him setting their homes on fire and killing their young men. He also saw how he would tear up pregnant women and kill their children. "**...their strong holds wilt thou set on fire, and their young men wilt thou slay with the sword, and wilt dash their children, and rip up their women with child.**"

I once laid hands on someone and immediately perceived the secular ambitions of the person. A voice kept stirring within me and saying, "What else do you want? What else do you crave for? What are you looking for in this life? Am I (the Lord) not enough for you?" The futility of this person's life as he focused on the world and all it had to offer was so strong upon me that I began to weep uncontrollably. I had not been thinking about those things but as soon as I laid hands on this person, my spirit was flooded with these thoughts and feelings. I was overwhelmed with this emotion and I wept pitifully over this fellow.

This is exactly what happened to Elisha. He was overwhelmed with the thoughts and feelings of what Hazael was going to become and do in the future.

... And when he (the Holy Spirit) is come, he will reprove (convince) ...

John 16:8

The Holy Spirit has the power to convict us of certain things. It is not a strange thing to break down emotionally under a strong conviction.

The LORD is exalted; for he dwelleth on high: he hath filled Zion with judgment and righteousness. And wisdom and knowledge shall be the stability of thy times, and strength of salvation: the fear of the LORD is his treasure.

Behold, their valiant ones shall cry without: the ambassadors of peace SHALL WEEP BITTERLY.

Isaiah 33:5-7

2. There are many examples of trembling in the Bible.

And he TREMBLING and astonished said, Lord, what wilt thou have me to do? And the Lord said unto him, Arise, and go into the city, and it shall be told thee what thou must do.

Acts 9:6

Fear ye not me? saith the LORD: WILL YE NOT TREMBLE at my presence, which have placed the sand for the bound of the sea by a perpetual decree, that it cannot pass it: and though the waves thereof toss themselves, yet can they not prevail; though they roar, yet can they not pass over it?

Jeremiah 5:22

WHEN I HEARD, MY BELLY TREMBLED; MY LIPS QUIVERED AT THE VOICE: rottenness entered into my bones, and I trembled in myself, that I might rest in the day of trouble: when he cometh up unto the people, he will invade them with his troops.

Habakuk 3:16

And he said unto me, O Daniel, a man greatly beloved, understand the words that I speak unto thee, and stand upright: for unto thee am I now sent. And when he had spoken this word unto me, I STOOD TREMBLING.

Daniel 10:11

3. There are many examples of SHAKING IN THE BIBLE.

And when they had prayed, THE PLACE WAS SHAKEN where they were assembled together; and they were all filled with the Holy Ghost, and they spake the word of God with boldness.

Acts 4:31

And suddenly there was a great earthquake, so that THE FOUNDATIONS OF THE PRISON WERE SHAKEN: and immediately all the doors were opened, and every one's bands were loosed.

Acts 16:26

There are a lot of shaking experiences recorded in the Bible. You will often find some kind of shaking experience when the Spirit of the Lord moved. Sometimes people trembled like leaves and at other times, there were earthquakes. Because these experiences are not arranged together in a list, they often go unnoticed. They are very much a part of the work of the Holy Spirit.

I have noticed how people shake, tremble and even convulse when the Holy Spirit is in manifestation. Is it any wonder if this frail human vessel trembles and shakes in the presence of the Almighty God?

It is easy to criticize these things from afar. However, when you experience the power you will realise how real it is. I remember interviewing a gentleman who was shaking uncontrollably.

I asked him, "Has this happened to you before?"

He said, "No, never."

He continued to shake and tremble uncontrollably.

"Are you surprised at what is happening?" I asked.

"Very surprised. I have always thought people were pretending and making things up but now I know it is real."

Dear friend, is it a strange thing if somebody trembles at the power of God?

Fear ye not me? saith the LORD: WILL YE NOT TREMBLE AT MY PRESENCE...

Jeremiah 5:22

4. Joy

Joy is a fruit of the Holy Spirit. When the Holy Spirit is in manifestation, there are sometimes demonstrations of joy. The obvious manifestations of joy are, smiling, laughing, dancing, running, jumping, clapping, singing and even crying.

You don't need to be very educated to know that these are expressions of joy. Should it be any wonder if you see any of these manifestations of joy because the Holy Spirit is at work?

Then Philip went down to the city of Samaria, and preached Christ unto them... And there was great JOY in that city.

Acts 8:5, 8

For the kingdom of God is not meat and drink; but righteousness, and peace, and JOY in the Holy Ghost.

Romans 14:17

Whom having not seen, ye love; in whom, though now ye see him not, yet believing, ye rejoice with JOY UNSPEAKABLE AND FULL OF GLORY:

1 Peter 1:8

Then was our mouth filled with LAUGHTER, and our tongue with singing: then said they among the heathen, The LORD hath done great things for them.

Psalm 126:2

Then he said unto them, Go your way, eat the fat, and drink the sweet, and send portions unto them for whom nothing is prepared: for this day is holy unto our Lord: neither be ye sorry; FOR THE JOY OF THE LORD is your strength.

Nehemiah 8:10

Speaking to yourselves in psalms and hymns and spiritual songs, SINGING and making melody in your heart to the Lord;

Ephesians 5:19

Don't be surprised if you see people laughing uncontrollably in the Holy Spirit. Don't criticize anyone if you see him or her running about in ecstasy. They are full of joy in the Holy Spirit. These are simply manifestations of the joy that is promised us in the Holy Spirit.

I remember watching a man of God as he ministered. He preached in a certain church for six weeks. Meetings took place every morning and evening. No matter what he was talking about people just started laughing. They just broke into uncontrollable laughter and received the Holy Spirit as he preached.

The Bible says, "When the Lord turned again the captivity of Zion, we were like them that dream. Then was our mouth filled with laughter..." (Psalm 126: 1, 2).

It is wonderful to see laughter in the Holy Spirit. It is a wonder. I see God anointing you with holy laughter!

Joy Brings Strength

The joy of the Lord is your strength. When you are down and depressed, you are weak. Depression is the loss of hope. It is depression that makes people think of killing themselves. When you have lost hope in an extreme way, you begin to think of killing yourself. You want to die because there is no hope. God wants to give us a revival of joy in the Holy Spirit!

5. Being Struck Dumb

And, behold, thou shalt be dumb, and not able to speak, until the day that these things shall be performed, because thou believest not my words, which shall be fulfilled in their season...

And his mouth was opened immediately, and his tongue loosed, and he spake, and praised God.

And fear came on all that dwelt round about them: and all these sayings were noised abroad throughout all the hill country of Judaea. And all they that heard them laid them up in their hearts, saying, What manner of child shall this be! And the hand of the Lord was with him.

Luke 1:20, 64-66

Another manifestation of the Holy Spirit is when He strikes you dumb. Zechariah was struck dumb for a while because He did not believe the angel.

Once, I remember when Kenneth Hagin was struck dumb right in the middle of his message. He became speechless and could not finish his message. We all sat there in amazement, as Brother Hagin stood speechless for over twenty minutes.

God is just showing us that the Holy Spirit is here. He is invisible but He makes Himself visible through these manifestations. This is what we call phanerosis: the making visible of the great invisible Holy Spirit.

6. Being Struck Blind

Paul was struck blind. Interestingly, Paul experienced several manifestations of the Spirit during his conversion experience.

There was a "falling to the ground".

There was "trembling".

There was an experience of "being struck blind".

And when we were all FALLEN to the earth, I heard a voice speaking unto me, and saying in the Hebrew tongue, Saul, Saul, why persecutest thou me? it is hard for thee to kick against the pricks.

Acts 26:14

And he TREMBLING and astonished said, Lord, what wilt thou have me to do? And the Lord said unto him, Arise, and go into the city, and it shall be told thee what thou must do. And the men which journeyed with him stood speechless, hearing a voice, but seeing no man.

And Saul arose from the earth; and WHEN HIS EYES WERE OPENED, HE SAW NO MAN: but they led him

115

by the hand, and brought him into Damascus. And he was three days without sight, and neither did eat nor drink.

And Ananias went his way, and entered into the house; and putting his hands on him said, Brother Saul, the Lord, even Jesus, that appeared unto thee in the way as thou camest, hath sent me, that thou mightest receive thy sight, and be filled with the Holy Ghost.

Acts 9:6-9, 17

7. Screaming

And they were astonished at his doctrine: for he taught them as one that had authority, and not as the scribes. And Jesus rebuked him, saying, Hold thy peace, and come out of him. And when the unclean spirit had torn him, and CRIED WITH A LOUD VOICE, he came out of him.

Mark 1:22, 25-26

Then Philip went down to the city of Samaria, and preached Christ unto them. And the people with one accord gave heed unto those things which Philip spake, hearing and seeing the miracles which he did. For unclean spirits, CRYING WITH LOUD VOICE, came out of many that were possessed with them: and many taken with palsies, and that were lame, were healed. And there was great joy in that city.

Acts 8:5-8

Do not be surprised when you see screaming, shouting, and crying people lying on the floor in a service in which the Holy Spirit is in full manifestation. I would prefer to be like Jesus than to follow the dictates of some stiff and over-righteous Christians. Jesus had screaming manifestations and so will I.

8. Heat and Burning

I indeed baptize you with water unto repentance: but he that cometh after me is mightier than I, whose shoes I am

not worthy to bear: he shall baptize you with the Holy
Ghost, and with FIRE:

Matthew 3:11

John answered, saying unto them all, I indeed baptize you
with water; but one mightier than I cometh, the latchet of
whose shoes I am not worthy to unloose: he shall baptize
you with the Holy Ghost and with FIRE:

Luke 3:16

To baptise with water means to pour water on you or to put
you into water. To baptise with fire means to pour fire on you or
to put you into fire. If you are baptised with water, you will feel
cold and wet. It is quite clear that if you are baptised with fire,
you will feel some heat.

I have heard different people testify of a burning sensation
or the feeling of "heat" all over their bodies. I have also heard
people testify of feeling heat on specific parts of their bodies.
Usually, these experiences indicate that the Lord is baptising you
with fire. Many times, people are experiencing healing when
they feel the baptism or pouring on of fire.

I remember a time I used to feel heat and a burning sensation
in one of my hands. This was a strange experience to me because
it kept recurring and I didn't know what it meant. This experience
of heat in my hand kept recurring. Looking back, I realise that
it was the period of time when I began to operate in the healing
ministry. I believe God was baptising or putting fire on me and
that is why I was feeling this heat in my hand. After God has
baptised you with fire, you will be able to walk in the anointing
that destroys the yoke.

And there appeared unto them cloven tongues like as
of fire, and it sat upon each of them. And they were all
filled with the Holy Ghost, and began to speak with other
tongues, as the Spirit gave them utterance.

Acts 2:3-4

Have Faith that This Is That!

When the Holy Spirit arrived on the day of Pentecost, there was a great uproar in the city. Some people thought that the people speaking in tongues were drunk. Others thought that the disciples were mad. I am sure there was a large group of people who just didn't know what was happening.

Apostle Peter, at the Lord's prompting, rose up in the midst of the confusion and boldly declared, "This is that!" What did he mean by "this is that"?

> But Peter, standing up with the eleven, lifted up his voice, and said unto them, Ye men of Judaea, and all ye that dwell at Jerusalem, be this known unto you, and hearken to my words:
>
> For these are not drunken, as ye suppose, seeing it is but the third hour of the day. But THIS IS THAT which was spoken by the prophet Joel...
>
> Acts 2:14-16

This is that which was spoken of by the Prophet Joel. One of the greatest keys to flowing in the supernatural is to believe that what you are seeing is what you have been trusting God for. Peter could have doubted that he was seeing what the Prophet Joel had spoken of. Instead, he boldly declared that he was seeing the supernatural.

The Prophet Eli had to point out to Samuel this same truth. He had to tell Samuel, "This is that!" The voice you are hearing is the Holy Spirit. When you have "this is that" faith, you will be able to accept the supernatural happenings in your life. When you hear the voice of the Spirit speaking to your mind, you will no longer say that it is just a thought.

One time while I was ministering, a young lady began to scream, twist and squirm. She had to be held down by four strong men. As I ministered to her, she suddenly became still and collapsed to the ground. I wondered to myself, "What has happened now?" The Holy Spirit said to me, "This is that!" This is Acts 8:5-8 reenacted.

> Then Philip went down to the city of Samaria, and preached Christ unto them. And the people with one accord gave heed unto those things which Philip spake, hearing and seeing the miracles which he did.
> For unclean spirits, crying with loud voice, came out of many that were possessed with them: and many taken with palsies, and that were lame, were healed. And there was great joy in that city.
>
> Acts 8:5-8

That was a sign of evil spirits coming out of people, screaming and tearing them to the ground. This is what occurred, after Jesus prayed for someone oppressed by an unclean spirit.

> And they brought him [the child] unto him: and when he saw him, straightway THE SPIRIT TARE HIM; AND HE FELL ON THE GROUND, AND WALLOWED FOAMING.
> And he asked his father, How long is it ago since this came unto him?
> And he said, Of a child. And ofttimes it hath cast him into the fire, and into the waters, to destroy him: but if thou canst do any thing, have compassion on us, and help us.
> Jesus said unto him, If thou canst believe, all things are possible to him that believeth.
> And straightway the father of the child cried out, and said with tears, Lord, I believe; help thou mine unbelief.
> When Jesus saw that the people came running together, he rebuked the foul spirit, saying unto him, Thou dumb and deaf spirit, I charge thee, come out of him, and enter no more into him.
> And the spirit cried, and rent him sore, and came out of him: and he was as one dead, insomuch that many said, He is dead.
>
> Mark 9:20-27

After ministering to a young boy, he screamed, convulsed and fell down as though dead. What was happening? Some modern analysts would have said, "This is post-ictal sleep. This is a temporary relief." But Jesus said, "This is it. He is healed."

We Had Cast out All but One

Many years ago I was involved in casting out thirty-six demons from a young student. For four hours, we struggled, trying to deliver the girl from evil powers. Of the thirty-six demons, all had been cast out with the exception of the last one. We commanded the spirit to go out but somehow we could never bring ourselves to believe that this girl had actually been delivered.

An older and experienced Christian was called in. After arriving, he said to the spirit, "I command you to come out in the name of Jesus." After that he asked the girl (just as we had been doing), "What is your name?" She responded normally just as she had been responding to us. He then turned to us and said, "She is alright."

"What!" I thought, "Is that all?"

You see, this older Christian believed that this was it! This was the deliverance! She was free. Her freedom was proved in the weeks following.

Does It Only Happen to Women?

PROVE ALL THINGS; hold fast that which is good.
1 Thessalonians 5:21

Accept supernatural things but prove them. Flow with them, but test them. I like to call people and ask them, "How come you fell under the power when I prayed for you?"

During one miracle service, I asked a pastor, "Have you ever fallen under the power?"

"Yes!" he answered.

"Were you surprised?" I asked.

"Very much!"

"Why were you surprised?"

He laughed and said, "I thought it only happened to women." He continued, "When you called me forward to pray for me, I said to myself that this thing will never happen to me." I came up there with a posture of resisting any such fall. But before I could realize it, I was on the floor."

If It's Real, It's Real!

One lady told me, "You have prayed for me many times and I have never fallen under the power. I didn't believe much in it." I myself could sense that she didn't believe much in the power of God. When you lay hands on people you can sometimes tell whether they are receiving or not. When it got to this lady's turn to be prayed for, the power of God went through her and she fell to the ground.

She told me later, "I was so surprised."

I asked her to stand up again and I prayed for her a second time. She fell right to the ground like a domino. I sensed that she was surprised so I wanted her to be doubly sure that the power of God was real. I prayed for her the third time. She crumbled to the ground for the third time.

Then I asked the ushers to lift her up again.

She told me later, "After the third time I decided that this will never happen again!"

"I will not allow myself to fall again."

I didn't know what was going on in her mind, but I decided to pray for her again. As soon as my hand touched her, she crumpled vertically to the ground. She lay on the ground as someone unconscious for several minutes. She was carried to her seat, helpless, under the power of God.

My friend, the supernatural is real. When you move out of natural, human thinking, you will begin to receive and experience the supernatural power of God.

How John Wesley Experienced Phanerosis

John Wesley was born in 1703 and died in 1771. He is probably the most well-known of all revival preachers. Wesley, a brilliant Oxford fellow and lecturer was converted at age thirty-five and went on to become the founder of the Methodist Movement. John Wesley experienced almost all the same phenomena that are taking place today. In April 1739, Wesley preached at Newgate Prison in Bristol. Wesley records that as he was preaching:

ONE, AND ANOTHER, AND ANOTHER SUNK TO THE EARTH: THEY DROPPED ON EVERY SIDE as if thunderstruck. One of them cried aloud. We besought God on her behalf and He turned her heaviness into joy. A second being in the same agony, we called upon God for her also; and He spoke peace unto her soul...

The next day a doctor who suspected trickery or fraud accompanied Wesley to the prison to see for Himself. He closely observed a woman who:

Broke out into STRONG CRIES AND TEARS. He went and stood close to her and observed every symptom, till great drops of sweat ran down her face, and ALL HER BONES SHOOK. He then knew not what to think, being clearly convinced it was not fraud, nor yet any natural disorder. But when both soul and body were healed in a moment, he acknowledged the finger of God.

Wesley notes:

Many more were brought to the berth. All were in floods of tears, cried, prayed, roared aloud, ALL OF THEM LYING ON THE GROUND. When I began to pray, the flame broke out. MANY CRIED aloud, MANY SANK to the ground, many trembled exceedingly.

Throughout his life, Wesley witnessed such incredible revival phenomena that even though his preaching was the tool God used, he was continually amazed. In an entry in his journal on July 29, 1759, Wesley records a number of examples that occurred while preaching:

SEVERAL FELL TO THE GROUND, some of whom seemed dead, others in the agonies of death, the violence of their BODILY CONVULSIONS EXCEEDING ALL DESCRIPTION... a child, seven years old, sees many visions and astonished the neighbours with her innocent, awful manner of declaring them.

Describing the same meeting, Wesley detailed how the power of God then moved out into the churchyard. The people were affected in ways that were beyond what he could describe. One man was "wounded by the Lord" while others tried to hold him up:

HIS OWN SHAKING EXCEEDED THAT OF A CLOTH IN THE WIND. It seemed as if the Lord came upon him like a giant, taking him by the neck and shaking all his bones in pieces...ANOTHER ROARED AND SCREAMED... some continued long as if they were dead, but with a calm sweetness in their looks. I SAW ONE WHO LAY TWO OR THREE HOURS IN THE OPEN AIR, and being then carried into the house, continued insensible another hour, as if actually dead. The first sign of life she showed was a rapture of praise intermixed with a small, joyous laughter...

Four days later:

While I prayed with them many crowded into the house, SOME OF WHOM BURST IN TO A STRANGE, INVOLUNTARY LAUGHTER, so that my voice could scarce be heard, and when I strove to speak louder a sudden hoarseness seized me. THEN THE LAUGHTER INCREASED...

A week later Wesley wrote:

I have generally observed more or less of these outward symptoms to attend the beginning of a general work of God. So it was in New England, Scotland, Holland, Ireland and many parts of England...

How Jonathan Edwards Experienced
Phanerosis

Jonathan Edwards was born in 1703 and died in 1758. Seminary professor Richard Lovelace believes "Jonathan Edward may well be the greatest American theologian and philosopher – and perhaps also the greatest mind – that America has yet produced." Edwards had first-hand experience with the manifestations of the Holy Spirit and became the chief spokesperson for the work of revival, trying to bridge the difficult chasm of emotional excess and freedom of the Spirit as evidenced with phenomena. Edward's wife, Sarah, a mother of eleven children, experienced her own major visitation from God and was incapacitated for seventeen days. Edwards supported and blessed the graces of God in both his wife and others.

*It was a very frequent thing to see **A HOUSE FULL OF OUTCRIES, FAINTING, CONVULSIONS**, and such like, both with distresses and also with admiration and joy.*

*It was not the manner here to hold meetings all night, as in some places, nor was it common to continue them till very late in the night; but it was pretty often so, **THAT THERE WERE SOME THAT WERE SO AFFECTED**, and their bodies so overcome, that **THEY COULD NOT GO HOME**, but were obliged to stay all night where they were ... and there were some instances of persons lying in a sort of trance, **REMAINING PERHAPS FOR A WHOLE TWENTY-FOUR HOURS MOTIONLESS**, and with their senses locked up; but in the meantime under strong imaginations, as though they went to heaven and had there a vision of glorious and delightful objects.*

But when the people were raised to this height, Satan took advantage, and his interposition, in many instances, soon became very apparent: and a great deal of caution and pains were found necessary to keep the people, many of them, from running wild.

CHAPTER 14

How the Names of God Release the Power of God

God has always introduced Himself by different names. Why does He do this? To show different aspects of Himself! These different names explain the different dimensions of God's power.

Different names are used for the Lord in the Bible. He introduced Himself as El Shaddai to Abraham. On another occasion, He introduced Himself to Abraham as Jehovah Jireh. Then He introduced Himself to Moses as I am that I am. On another occasion, He introduced Himself to Moses as Jehovah Rophe. Yet again, He introduced Himself as Jehovah Shalom to Gideon. Each time God introduced Himself by a different name He did different things.

You may call a man you know your brother, your father, your uncle, your friend, your husband, your colleague, your partner or your buddy. Each of these titles reflects a different kind of relationship. Each of these titles reflects a different experience that you have with the same person. It is important to get to know God by His different names. If you get to know God as El Shaddai, you will know Him as the all-providing and all-sufficient God. If you get to know God as Jehovah Rophe, you will experience Him as a healer. God is many things and it is up to us to develop our faith to receive God in His different roles.

Twelve Names of God

1. Elohim

> In the beginning God (**ELOHIM**) created the heaven and the earth.
>
> Genesis 1:1

In the very beginning of the Bible, God's name is mentioned repeatedly. The name of God that is used in Genesis Chapter One is "*Elohim*". *Elohim* describes God as the Creator. Creativity is an aspect of God's character. Man's creative ability is from God. The power of invention is God-given. When man was created in the image of God, he was also blessed with God's creative nature. The creation story therefore reveals God's creative nature.

2. El Shaddai

> And when Abram was ninety years old and nine, the Lord appeared to Abram, and said unto him, I am the Almighty God (EL SHADDAI); walk before me, and be thou perfect.
>
> Genesis 17:1

Later on in the Bible, we see God introducing Himself to Abraham as El Shaddai.

The name of God used in this Scripture is "*El Shaddai*". *El Shaddai* means "the mighty one with a lot of breasts", or "the mighty breasted one". You see, the breast meets every need of the baby. It is the baby's meat, cereal, vitamins, minerals, milk, porridge and drinking water. A baby on breast milk does not need to take in anything else. So when God introduced Himself to Abraham as *El Shaddai*, He was saying that, "I'm the Almighty One who has everything that you will ever need." I see God giving you all that you will ever need!

3. Jehovah

And God spake unto Moses, and said unto him, I am the Lord: And I appeared unto Abraham, unto Isaac, and unto Jacob, by the name of God Almighty, but by my name JEHOVAH was I not known to them.

Exodus 6:2-3

Later, God confirms the name "Jehovah", the Hebrew "*YHWH*", which is the equivalent of "I am", the promise-keeper, to Moses.

His name "*Jehovah*" is combined with other words to reveal the many aspects of His promise-keeping nature and the different ways He fulfils His promises.

4. I Am That I Am

And Moses said unto God, Behold, when I come unto the children of Israel, and shall say unto them, The God of your fathers hath sent me unto you; and they shall say to me, What is his name? what shall I say unto them? And God said unto Moses, **I AM THAT I AM (EHAYEH ASHER EHAYEH)**: and he said, Thus shalt thou say unto the children of Israel, I AM hath sent me unto you.

Exodus 3: 13-14

At another time, we see God revealing Himself to Moses in a different way. He described Himself as, "I am that I am," which in Hebrew is "*Ehayeh Asher Ehayeh*".

"I am that I am" means "the God who is existing". But it also means "the Lord who keeps promises". God was going to bring Moses and the Israelites into the Promised Land and He was telling him, "I'm the God who keeps covenants and makes agreements. I don't break my agreements."

We see God therefore in the Scriptures, introducing Himself in different ways as different situations came up.

5. Jehovah Nissi: The Lord Our Banner

And Moses built an altar, and called the name of it **JEHOVAH NISSI**: "For he said, because the LORD hath sworn that the LORD will have war with Amalek from generation to generation.

Exodus 17:15-16

When you know God as Jehovah Nissi, you know Him as the victorious one who is a banner over you in all your battles. God will help you to fight and win the war of ministry.

6. Jehovah Jireh: The Lord Will See or Provide

And Abraham said, My son, God will provide himself a lamb for a burnt offering: so they went both of them together.
And they came to the place which God had told him of; and Abraham built an altar there, and laid the wood in order, and bound Isaac his son, and laid him on the altar upon the wood. And Abraham stretched forth his hand, and took the knife to slay his son.
And the angel of the LORD called unto him out of heaven, and said, Abraham, Abraham: and he said, Here am I.
And he said, Lay not thine hand upon the lad, neither do thou any thing unto him: for now I know that thou fearest God, seeing thou hast not withheld thy son, thine only son from me.
And Abraham lifted up his eyes, and looked, and behold behind him a ram caught in a thicket by his horns: and Abraham went and took the ram, and offered him up for a burnt offering in the stead of his son.
And Abraham called the name of that place **JEHOVAH JIREH**: as it is said to this day, In the mount of the LORD it shall be seen.

Genesis 22:8-14

Abraham encountered God as a provider. In recent years, the church of God had experienced God as Jehovah Jireh, the provider of wealth and material blessings. Unfortunately, these material blessings have also led to the backsliding of the church. There is no doubt that in years past the church did not know God as a provider. We saw God as someone who wanted us to be poor and to suffer loss in all areas. Through the teaching on prosperity the church has opened herself up to accept God as a provider, Jehovah Jireh.

7. Jehovah Shalom: The Lord Our Peace

And Gideon went in, and made ready a kid, and unleavened cakes of an ephah of flour: the flesh he put in a basket, and he put the broth in a pot, and brought it out unto him under the oak, and presented it.

And the angel of God said unto him, Take the flesh and the unleavened cakes, and lay them upon this rock, and pour out the broth. And he did so. Then the angel of the LORD put forth the end of the staff that was in his hand, and touched the flesh and the unleavened cakes; and there rose up fire out of the rock, and consumed the flesh and the unleavened cakes. Then the angel of the LORD departed out of his sight. And when Gideon perceived that he was an angel of the LORD, Gideon said, Alas, O Lord God! for because I have seen an angel of the LORD face to face."

And the LORD said unto him, Peace be unto thee; fear not: thou shalt not die.

Then Gideon built an altar there unto the LORD, and called it **JEHOVAH SHALOM**: unto this day it is yet in Ophrah of the Abiezrites.

Judges 6:19-24

Gideon, who judged Israel, came to know the Lord as someone who brought peace into his life. Some people are unable to live at peace with each other even though they are Christians. They may know God as a provider of riches and wealth but not as someone who brings peace into their lives.

It is important to put aside conflict even though you may come from a tribe or nation that is always in conflict with others.

God is a God of peace. You must get to know Him as Jehovah Shalom.

8. Jehovah Tsidqenuw: The Lord Our Righteousness

In his days Judah shall be saved, and Israel shall dwell safely: and this is his name whereby he shall be called, **THE LORD OUR RIGHTEOUSNESS (JEHOVAH TSIDQENUW)**.

Jeremiah 23:6

God is a righteous God and it is important to know Him as the one who makes you righteous. There is none righteous, no not one. Except the Lord make us righteous through the blood of Jesus, we remain in our filth.

9. Jehovah Sabaoth: The Lord of Hosts

And this man went up out of his city yearly to worship and to sacrifice unto **the LORD OF HOSTS (JEHOVAH SABAOTH)** in Shiloh. And the two sons of Eli, Hophni and Phinehas, the priests of the Lord, were there.

1 Samuel 1:3

When you grow in the ministry, you will recognize that ministry is just a war. The Lord of hosts is the commander of the armies of the Lord. He is a soldier and He understands war. When you grow in your understanding and your commitment to the will of God, you will find yourself experiencing God as a leader of His armies, with you as one of His principal soldiers.

10. Jehovah Shammah: The Lord Is Present

And the gates of the city shall be after the names of the tribes of Israel: three gates northward; one gate of Reuben, one gate of Judah, one gate of Levi.

And at the east side four thousand and five hundred: and three gates; and one gate of Joseph, one gate of Benjamin, one gate of Dan.

And at the south side four thousand and five hundred

measures: and three gates; one gate of Simeon, one gate of Issachar, one gate of Zebulun.

At the west side four thousand and five hundred, with their three gates; one gate of Gad, one gate of Asher, one gate of Naphtali.

It was round about eighteen thousand measures: and the name of the city from that day shall be, **THE LORD IS THERE (JEHOVAH SHAMMAH)**.

Ezekiel 48:31-35

To experience the presence of the Lord is a great and important thing. The presence of the Lord is often the only sign you can look out for to know when someone is walking with God. You must grow up and begin to know God as someone who is really present in a demonstrable way. Few people know God as Jehovah Shammah. They may know Him as Jehovah Jireh or El Shaddai. But few people know His presence.

11. Jehovah Rohi: The Lord Our Shepherd

The LORD is my shepherd **(JEHOVAH ROHI)**; I shall not want

Psalms 23:1

Knowing the Lord as a shepherd is to know the Lord as a guide, a comforter and a leader. Many people are not led by the Lord in a personal way. God can lead you every day and show you where to go, what to say and what to do. Knowing God as Jehovah Rohi and learning to be led by the Spirit is perhaps the most important skill every Christian must have. I recommend God to you as Jehovah Rohi: the one who leads you like a shepherd.

12. Jehovah Rophe: The Lord Our Healer

And said, If thou wilt diligently hearken to the voice of the Lord thy God, and wilt do that which is right in his sight, and wilt give ear to his commandments, and keep all his statutes, I will put none of these diseases upon thee, which

I have brought upon the Egyptians: for I am **THE LORD THAT HEALETH THEE (JEHOVAH ROPHE)**

Exodus 15:26

Finally, we come to Jehovah as a healer. We have known Him as a provider of money, finances and resources. We have known Him as a guide. We have known Him as a shepherd. We have known His presence. We have known Him as a creator. We have known Him as a commander of armies. We have known Him as someone who gives us peace in this life. It is now time to know Him as a healer.

As the Lord was bringing the Israelites out of Egypt, He shocked them by introducing Himself to them as a physician, a specialist and a healer. What a shock! When you know God as a healer you can minister to people like Jesus did. Jesus is not just a Jesus who teaches. He is a Jesus who heals, He is a healing Jesus: Jehovah Rophe!

How to Receive from Jehovah Rophe

When God saved His people Israel from Egypt, He introduced Himself to them as "the Lord that healeth thee". The Hebrew words for the phrase "God that healeth thee," are "*Jehovah Rophe.*"

The name "*Jehovah Rophe*" means, "the Lord your doctor", "the Lord your physician", or "the Lord your healer".

When God introduced Himself here in Exodus, He was saying, "Let me show you a new aspect of myself; let me show you another side of my nature. I am Jehovah the physician, a specialist." He is the Lord your healer and your specialist!

When we speak of healing, most of us think of physical ailments only. However, there are many areas in our lives that need healing. God wants to heal every aspect of our lives. He wants to come into our lives as Jehovah the specialist. So what does "*Rophe*" mean? "*Rophe*" is a Hebrew word that means "to heal", or "to repair".

Seven Dimensions of Jehovah Rophe

1. *"Rophe"* means **"to prevent disease"**.

Jehovah Rophe said He would prevent the diseases that are on the Egyptians, from coming on Israel. The ability to be alive is from the Lord. If you find yourself alive, you must know that it is God who has allowed you to be here. The breath in you, my brother, is from the Lord. It is God who keeps you from getting sick. If you don't get a particular disease, it means that *Jehovah Rophe*, the Lord that healeth thee, has prevented you from getting that disease!

2. *"Rophe"* means **"to heal."**

"To heal", means *"to become or make something healthy again"*, *"to cure somebody who is ill"*, *"to make someone feel happy again"*, *"to put an end to something or make something easier to bear."*

It means *"to heal and to restore health."* This is what Jehovah Rophe does for you.

Many diseases have no physical cure, especially diseases that have to do with the mind and the emotions. God is able to heal the complex burdens of the human race.

As you can see, "to heal" also means, *"to make someone feel happy again"*. It also means to make something easier to bear. This amazing dictionary definition of the word "to heal" opens up many new dimensions to the healing ministry. God will make you happy again.

3. *"Rophe"* means **"to repair."**

"To repair", means *"to mend something that is broken, damaged or torn"*; it also means *"to say or do something in order to improve a bad or unpleasant situation"*.

When God revealed Himself as Jehovah Rophe, He was saying that "I am the Lord that repairs". You may regret some of your actions and wish that things hadn't happened the way they did. But God is introducing Himself as the one who can repair. God desires to repair his damaged and blotched handiwork. He wants to repair broken men and restore them. This is because men are the crowning glory of His work. God has pledged to completely repair the Earth and the creation.

4. *"Rophe"* means **"to restore."**

"To restore", means *"to bring back a situation or a feeling that existed before"* or *"to bring something back to a former condition, place or position"*. When God manifests as Jehovah Rophe, He will bring back a feeling of well-being.

5. *"Rophe"* means **"to mend."**

"To mend", means *"to repair something that has been damaged or broken so that it can be used again"*, or *"to improve in health after being sick"*. God is repairing your life so that you can be used again for His glory. God is repairing your broken life and your damaged relationships for His glory.

6. *"Rophe"* means **"to fix."**

"To fix", means "to repair or correct something".

Jehovah Rophe means, *"I'm the Lord that mends every situation and the Lord that fixes things"*. Many of us have situations in our lives that need some fixing and adjusting. God introduces circumstances into our lives to adjust and to fix things.

I see the Lord correcting every crooked situation in your life.

7. *"Rophe"* means **"to cure."**

"To cure", means *"to make someone healthy again after an illness"*, and *"to make an illness go away"*. It also means, *"to deal with a problem successfully"*, or *"to stop somebody from behaving in a particular way, especially in a way that is bad"*.

God is in the process of making you healthy again. God is the one who has the power to make an illness go away and to deal with your problem successfully.

CHAPTER 15

Six Dimensions of Divine Healing

The Source of All Sickness

God put man in the Garden of Eden but things went the wrong way. Adam sinned and God had to apply His divine rules against Adam. This is because He is a just God who applies rules fairly and equally to all. This is unlike the justice of men that is often hypocritical and partial. Primitive governments apply the rules, laws and institutions of justice only to their enemies.

There are prisoners in jails everywhere who are praying for a change of government. They know that a new government will apply the laws differently and free them from prison. This is why many developing nations have little confidence in the courts of law.

God, however, is a just God who applied the rules evenly to His own creation. He said to them, "Now that you have crossed the line you can't stay here; you have to go out." That is why Adam had to leave the beautiful garden that God had made for him. As a result of the sin of disobedience, much of the Earth was destroyed and is still being destroyed.

This Earth will eventually be totally destroyed and be replaced with a new Heaven and a new Earth!

When sin entered into the lives of Adam and Eve, many changes took place. Adam was forced out of the garden and found himself at the mercy of the elements.

With sin now in their lives, death was at work in their bodies. People, who would never have grown old, began to grow old. Eyes, which would never have faded, began to fade. People, who would never have died, had to die. We would have lived forever! Adam and Eve then decided to make some clothes to protect themselves.

When the Lord came along, He saw the "leaf clothes" Adam had made and knew that these clothes would not last long. He helped them to make some clothes out of skin. This was God's first step to helping fallen mankind help themselves. God has been helping ever since. The wisdom to invent medicines is part of God's grace to help mankind. Every medical discovery is part of God's plan to rescue man from his own ways.

God then prepared a plan to redeem and rescue his creation. This rescue plan was to be executed through Christ the Redeemer. There were many predictions in the Old Testament about the coming Messiah who would heal and deliver. The coming of Christ to this Earth was predicted for years. This is one thing that separates Jesus from other leaders of all other religions. His coming, His purpose, His life and His death were predicted and described long before He came to earth.

Isaiah predicted that there would be someone who would take up our sorrows, our grief and the chastisement of our peace. He foretold that someone would come to take away the things that disturb our peace of mind in this life. This person would take up our sicknesses and bring us healing through His stripes.

Surely he hath borne our griefs, and carried our sorrows: yet we did esteem him stricken, smitten of God, and afflicted.

Isaiah 53:4

God has expressed in His Word over and over again, His heart's desire to heal His creation. He is very concerned with the repairing of His creation, which is lost to the devil.

Six Dimensions of Divine Healing

Divine healing is therefore healing that comes from God. This is in contrast to the healing that man engineers for himself. With our limited minds, we can see only sections of the problems of the human race. Many people do not appreciate the complex problems of the human race. There are several situations in our lives that need the touch of God. What is God trying to do through the healing ministry? What is He repairing and fixing?

Divine healing covers all the aspects of healing. The following is a short list of some of the aspects of divine healing.

1. Divine healing affects birth defects and genetic disorders.

And as Jesus passed by, he saw a man which was BLIND FROM HIS BIRTH. And his disciples asked him, saying, Master, who did sin, this man, or his parents, that he was born blind?

John 9:1-2

There are many illnesses we fight which are simply inherited from our fathers. For instance, diseases like hypertension, diabetes, asthma, sickle cell disease, mental disorders, mental retardation etc. are received effortlessly by children from their fathers and mothers. Through no fault of theirs, people wake up to the realities that they have inherited conditions and illnesses that they did not contribute to. In the ministry of Jesus, you find healings of conditions that existed from birth.

God's power of healing can save you from inherited illnesses.

2. Divine healing affects emotional illnesses.

The Spirit of the Lord is upon me, because he hath anointed me to preach the gospel to the poor; he hath sent me to HEAL THE BROKENHEARTED, to preach deliverance to the captives, and recovering of sight to the blind, to set at liberty them that are bruised,

Luke 4:18

Surprisingly, Jesus' reference to healing in this Scripture is not about healing heart failure (congestive cardiac failure) or heart attacks (cardiac arrest). Jesus' healing ministry specifically mentioned the healing of the broken-hearted.

The broken-hearted are people with emotional and psychological setbacks. To have a broken heart is to suffer from deep disappointment. To have a broken heart is to have a devastating experience that leaves a person without hope, faith or love. The Greek word for broken heart is "syntribo" and it means "to be shattered".

Our lives are full of shattered dreams and hopes. Christ came into the world to save men from their shattered dreams and aspirations.

He healeth the broken in heart, and bindeth up their wounds.

Psalm 147:3

What does it mean to have a broken heart? Broken hearts result from disappointments. Sometimes a man promises to marry a lady but disappoints her. This man may end up marrying someone else.

What you hoped would never happen is what has happened. But God can heal any disappointment and repair your heart.

God heals all our diseases and now He is saying that He is going to heal your soul. He's going to heal your inner man.

Many people are emotionally disturbed, and suffer from the disappointment and disillusionments of this life. That is why we need the Healing Jesus!

Did you know that the psychiatrist is the doctor with fewest answers? Almost every mental patient is given something to make him calm down and sleep. The psychiatrists know very little about why mental conditions develop. But God knows everything. He reaches to the innermost parts of our being and heals the broken hearted. "He restoreth my soul…" (Psalm 23:3).

I remember meeting a man who said, "I'll never trust another woman." He told me, "One day, I went out and came home unexpectedly in the middle of the night."

He said to me, "I found my wife in my bed with another man. Both of them were completely naked." He told me, "I exercised self-control, but I could have killed them both. I drove them out of the house without their clothes and called the police."

As I talked to this man, I realized that his heart was very disturbed. He described how he could not relate normally to women anymore. He hated all women and had decided never to get married. There are many men and women like this man. Totally discouraged, disappointed and disillusioned by what they have experienced in this life.

But God can give you healing and change you on the inside. The medicines that psychiatrists give often only sedate the patient or improve their mood. There is no real healing for the psychological and emotional problem. God can heal what man cannot heal!

He said, "I am the Lord your doctor, the Lord your healer, the Lord your physician." I am Jehovah Rophe!

3. Divine healing affects our behaviour.

And when he was come out of the ship, immediately there met him out of the tombs a man with an unclean

spirit, Who had his dwelling among the tombs; and no man could bind him, no, not with chains:

Mark 5:2-3

A psychiatry lecturer once said that most people have some amount of abnormal behaviour. Many people do not have full-blown mental illness but they do show some odd behaviour. Today, a whole range of words and definitions have been developed in order to adequately describe the varied levels of behavioural dysfunction. Some people are said to be eccentric, which is a polite description of an odd, queer, off-centre, erratic and strange person.

One of the commonest problems is fear or paranoia. Many fearful people live abnormal lives because of various fears they constantly entertain. Others are depressed to varying degrees at different times. Some people suffer from rage disorders, sexual disorders, personality disorders, delusions, hallucinations, mania, and ultimately schizophrenia, which is full-blown madness. Most of us live between the ranges of normalcy and full-blown madness.

Divine healing tackles the full range of problems that afflict us. Through the Word of God, we are saved from behavioural patterns that were useless and self-destructive.

4. Divine healing cures us from the effects of death.

...but the sorrow of the world worketh death.

2 Corinthians 7:10

When tragedy strikes, there is a sense of uneasiness and fear that is difficult to shake off. There is a sinking feeling that is difficult to get rid of. The heart is sick and broken when a loved one is suddenly and tragically plucked away. Only God can heal the futility, depression and heartache that are associated with death. Many people do not recover from the death of a loved one. Some live in constant bitterness and depression for the rest of their lives. Indeed, only God can heal such feelings of hopelessness and uselessness.

5. Divine healing cures us from the effects of futility.

Vanity of vanities, saith the Preacher, vanity of vanities; all is vanity.

Ecclesiastes 1:2

The uselessness of life is something that God takes away by His power and His anointing. Sometimes you look at life and ask what it's all about. You find yourself struggling and unhappy. We often think that when you get certain things like cars, marriage etc. everything will be okay.

However, every man will come to the same conclusion that Solomon did: vanity of vanities, all is vanity. Indeed all is vanity. Life on this Earth can be defined as building a series of sandcastles that are soon washed away. Have you ever wondered why rich western nations have the highest suicide rates? The emptiness and hollowness of riches stares them in the face and they know that Solomon was right. All is vanity. Many kill themselves because there is no meaning to this life.

God's power heals us of the futility of this life. God's power heals us from the sense of uselessness in our lives.

6. He will permanently heal the nations of the world.

And he shewed me a pure river of water of life, clear as crystal, proceeding out of the throne of God and of the Lamb.

In the midst of the street of it, and on either side of the river, was there the tree of life, which bare twelve manner of fruits, and yielded her fruit every month: and the leaves of the tree were FOR THE HEALING OF THE NATIONS.

Revelation 22:1-2

Many nations need healing. Rwanda needs healing and so does Burundi. Sierra Leone needs healing. During the civil war in Sierra Leone, rebels cut off the hands of many civilians. Many nations do not have electricity and running water. It is not only poor African countries that need healing. The nations of Israel and Palestine also need healing. America is divided along racial lines. Europe is plagued with disillusioned citizens who no longer believe in God. India and Pakistan fight constantly whilst many nations live with poverty, war and famine. North and South Korea live in constant tension. Egypt, Syria, Afghanistan and Iraq are bleeding every day with suicide bombs and constant instability.

Thank God that He has leaves that will heal these devastated nations. It is clear that no political, economic or military remedy can ever heal the nations of the world.

The leaves of the tree will be used to bring about a permanent healing for the nations.

CHAPTER 16

Why God Heals People Today

1. God heals so that His glory is revealed.

When Jesus heard that, he said, THIS SICKNESS IS NOT UNTO DEATH, BUT FOR THE GLORY OF GOD, that the Son of God might be glorified thereby.

John 11:4

This Scripture shows that God heals so that His glory is revealed. When we have miracles in the church, it is because God wants us to get glimpses of His glory. He wants us to see His power. He wants to show us that He is the Almighty God and that there is no problem too big for Him to solve.

I remember a man who had had a stroke and was paralyzed on one side. I did not even know that he was in the church service. This man had actually lost his job because of his paralysis. He was not even aware that the healing power of God was working in him. He just realized that he could move his leg and arm again when he waved at someone on his way home. The power of God had moved his body.

2. God heals so that His works will be manifested.

Jesus answered, Neither hath this man sinned, nor his parents: BUT THAT THE WORKS OF GOD SHOULD BE MADE MANIFEST IN HIM.

John 9:3

Sometimes the problems we have are going to lead to the greatest blessings in our lives. God is going to use that thing to bring a great miracle into your life.

I love to tell the story of a 31-year-old lady who received a powerful miracle healing. She got married in 1991, and had her first pregnancy in 1993 that turned out to be an ectopic pregnancy. She was operated upon and her right fallopian tube was cut off on the 1st of August 1993. She had a second pregnancy in 1994 and that was also an ectopic pregnancy but this time on the left side. She was operated on and part of the left tube was cut off (the doctors tried to save a part of the tube). In 1995, she had a third ectopic pregnancy! She was operated on and the doctors still tried to save the tube. In the first week of August 1996, she had a fourth ectopic pregnancy and this time the rest of the left tube was taken off. Her doctor then told her that the only way she could have a child was by a test-tube baby or by adoption.

A year later, during a Miracle Service I held at the Grace Bible Church - Soweto, South Africa, God did a wonderful miracle for Patricia. During the ministration, I asked all those who were sick to place their hands where their illnesses were. Patricia placed her hand on her stomach. Her husband was not sitting with her at that time so he ran to her to make sure she was praying. He thought she would not pray about their situation because it looked so hopeless.

Patricia said that she felt she was the only one being spoken to. She testified that when she placed her hand on her abdomen, she felt the power of God coming all over her. She said the sensation she felt was difficult to describe but she knew within herself at that moment, that God had touched her! The best description she could give of the healing power was a feeling of "sweet pain".

After this healing experience, she went to see her gynaecologist claiming that she was pregnant. She was driven away by the doctor who told her that she needed to see a psychiatrist! This doctor told her she was developing a mental problem because he knew it was not possible for her to get pregnant. But Patricia was so sure that she was pregnant, and she went to see other doctors. It was eventually proved that the impossible had happened: she was actually pregnant!

There is no medical explanation for this miracle because a woman cannot conceive normally if she does not have fallopian tubes.

When I returned to South Africa on the 26th of September, 1998 to hold another miracle service in the same church, an excited and overjoyed Patricia came up stage with her miracle baby, to give this testimony of what God had done for her. She named the child "Odirile", which means—"He (God) has made it"!

You know, just like the woman with the issue of blood, Patricia felt something. It is possible to feel the power of God and the unction of God. Somebody might ask, "What is that feeling like?" It is very much like a normal feeling because it is a feeling.

The supernatural and the natural are almost the same. I was preaching about the supernatural power when Patricia felt the anointing. When some people feel the anointing, they dismiss it as something natural. Open yourself to the supernatural and you will experience the power of God.

3.   God heals to confirm the preaching of His Word.

And these signs shall follow them that believe; In my name shall they cast out devils; they shall speak with new tongues; They shall take up serpents; and if they drink any deadly thing, it shall not hurt them; they shall lay hands on the sick, and they shall recover. So then

after the Lord had spoken unto them, he was received up into heaven, and sat on the right hand of God.

And they went forth, and preached everywhere, THE LORD WORKING WITH THEM, AND CONFIRMING THE WORD WITH SIGNS FOLLOWING. AMEN.

Mark 16:17-20

God heals to confirm the Word of God that has been preached. Miracles have a primary function of confirming the preaching of the Word of God. This is not the same as eradicating all the diseases in a community. Confirming and affirming a sermon preached by a pastor is quite different from eradicating polio, measles or small pox from a community. God is not trying to eradicate diseases from the community. God is in the business of confirming the messages that have been preached by His servants!

4. God heals in order to help people believe in Him.

Believe me that I am in the Father, and the Father in me: or else believe me for the very works' sake.

John 14:11

If I do not the works of my Father, believe me not. But if I do, though ye believe not me, believe the works: that ye may know, and believe, that the Father is in me, and I in him.

John 10:37-38

Some people just want to see a miracle so that they can believe. Such people just need a miracle to help them believe. When they see the work of God, they are utterly and totally convinced about the truth of the Word.

5. God does healing miracles in order to help people repent and change their ways.

Miracles are also given to help people repent and come to the Lord. This is why Jesus rebuked the cities where He did His mighty works. His mighty works were intended to help them repent from their evil ways.

Then began he to upbraid the cities wherein most of his mighty works were done, because they repented not:
Matthew 11:20

6.   **God does miracles to show approval of His servants.**

Ye men of Israel, hear these words; Jesus of Nazareth, A MAN APPROVED OF GOD AMONG YOU BY MIRACLES AND WONDERS AND SIGNS, which God did by him in the midst of you, as ye yourselves also know:
Acts 2:22

Jesus answered them, I told you, and ye believed not: the works that I do in my Father's name, they bear witness of me.
John 10:25

God does miracles, signs and wonders to show his approval of the person who is preaching. God is not trying to make pastors into doctors. He is not trying to use the evangelist to eradicate malaria, sickle cell disease, hypertension, and diabetes from the community. He does miracles to show His approval of His servants.

These miracles have specific purposes. God is showing His approval of His servants through the miracles. How did God approve of Jesus Christ of Nazareth? He approved of Him by miracles, wonders and signs. That is the way God approves of His servant. This is what the Bible says.

I've been at places, where God approved of me with signs and wonders. I remember when I heard the voice of the Holy Spirit speaking to my heart. He said to me, "Today, I will honour you." The Lord did such wonderful miracles at that place. He did this because I was surrounded by people who did not really believe in me.

Jesus preached the Word. He said He was the Bread of Life; The Way, The Truth and The Life. God approved of Him and showed that He was speaking the truth by performing signs and wonders.

This also explains why people fall under the power. Falling under the power is a sign. People love miracles. People love a display of power. The display of power shows God's approval of the man of God. They know that anyone can shout up a sermon but it is not that easy to conjure a miracle.

7. **God does miracles in order to destroy the works of the devil.**

    He that committeth sin is of the devil; for the devil sinneth from the beginning. For this purpose the Son of God was manifested, that he might destroy the works of the devil.

    1 John 3:8

    You need to understand that there is a devil that rules this world. This is obvious when you look at the chaos in the world.

    The dictators that are imposed on different nations, the wickedness in the world, the inequalities of our society, the starvation, the hunger, the sickness, the diseases and the sufferings of many people prove that the overall ruler is a very wicked person. The Bible calls him the "god of this world".

    In whom the god of this world hath blinded the minds of them which believe not, lest the light of the glorious gospel of Christ, who is the image of God, should shine unto them.

    2 Corinthians 4:4

    There is a song we used to sing: *He's got the whole world in his hands, He's got the whole wide world in his hands; He's got the whole world in his hands, He's got the whole world in his hands.*

The words of this song cannot be true because the Bible clearly says that Satan is the god of this world. The devil also claims that the kingdoms of this world had been handed over to him:

And the devil, taking him up into an high mountain, shewed unto him all the kingdoms of the world in a moment of time.

And the devil said unto him, All this power will I give thee, and the glory of them: for that is delivered unto me; and to whomsoever I will I give it. If thou therefore wilt worship me, all shall be thine.

Luke 4:5-7

Some of the kingdoms in this world are Ghana, England, America, Iran, Kosovo, Iraq, Sierra Leone, Israel, Nigeria, Liberia, Cameroon, Angola, and India. The devil showed Jesus some of these kingdoms. Jesus refused to bow to the devil and so He was not given the control of the nations of the world. They stayed firmly in the clutches of the devil.

God is Almighty and reigns over all things. However, the devil is the one that specifically controls this earthly world now. He said He could give it to whomsoever He would. This is why Germany for instance, may be developed but there is also a lot of unhappiness among the people. That is why Switzerland may have a lot of money but with a lot of pain, sorrow and depression.

Of course we know that one day the kingdoms of this world will "…become the kingdoms of our Lord and of his Christ and he shall reign for ever and ever" (Revelation 11:15).

The devil is the one ruling the world today. He causes the diseases and the sicknesses in this world. Jesus cast out devils from many of the people that He healed. So many problems are caused by the devil. Until you get to the root of the problem you often do not get them solved.

This is why Jesus is in the healing business. This is why we believe in healing. We can never stop believing in healing.

I want to encourage you to believe in miracles because miracles are real. Jesus is the Sun of righteousness with healing in His wings.

8. **God does miracles to announce the arrival of the Kingdom of God.**

    And as ye go, preach, saying, The kingdom of heaven is at hand. Heal the sick, cleanse the lepers, raise the dead, cast out devils: freely ye have received, freely give.

    Matthew 10:7-8

9. **God does miracles so that more people will attend church and follow the Word of God.**

    And a great multitude followed him, because they saw his miracles which he did on them that were diseased.

    John 6:2

150

CHAPTER 17

Why God Does Not Heal Everyone

1. God does not heal everyone because some people believe when they see miracles.

   Then many (not all) of the Jews which came to Mary, and had seen the things which Jesus did, believed on him.

   John 11:45

2. God does not heal everyone because only a few people believe in God when they see miracles.

   But though he had done so many miracles before them, yet they believed not on him:

   John 12:37

It would be nice if there were many more miracles but the fact is that miracles are only going to add a few more people to the faith. Some people do not believe no matter what they see. You can raise the dead in front of them and they will still not believe. Abraham told the rich man: "... If they hear not Moses and the prophets, neither will they be persuaded, though one rose from the dead" (Luke 16:31).

In fact, some people will hate you because of the miracles they see.

Then again the Pharisees also asked him how he had received his sight. He said unto them, He put clay upon mine eyes, and I washed, and do see.

Therefore said some of the Pharisees, This man is not of God, because he keepeth not the sabbath day. Others said, How can a man that is a sinner do such miracles? And there was a division among them.

They say unto the blind man again, What sayest thou of him, that he hath opened thine eyes? He said, He is a prophet.

But the Jews did not believe concerning him, that he had been blind, and received his sight, until they called the parents of him that had received his sight.

And they asked them, saying, Is this your son, who ye say was born blind? how then doth he now see? His parents answered them and said, We know that this is our son, and that he was born blind:

But by what means he now seeth, we know not; or who hath opened his eyes, we know not: he is of age; ask him: he shall speak for himself.

These words spake his parents, because they feared the Jews: for the Jews had agreed already, that if any man did confess that he was Christ, he should be put out of the synagogue.

Therefore said his parents, He is of age; ask him. Then again called they the man that was blind, and said unto him, Give God the praise: we know that this man is a sinner.

He answered and said, Whether he be a sinner or no, I know not: one thing I know, that, whereas I was blind, now I see.

John 9:15-25

The miracle Jesus did brought about a surprising division. You would have thought that the healing of a man born blind would make everybody believe.

If God was trying to make everybody believe by miracles then He failed. No matter what God does, certain people will never believe. God is therefore not in a hurry to heal everyone.

I know a man of God who had a halo appear over his head when he was preaching. Do you think that everybody believed in his ministry? Certainly not! We must understand then that miracles or no miracles, the work of God still goes on. Only some people will believe because of the miracles.

This explains why one of the greatest evangelists of our time, Billy Graham, could preach the gospel without praying for miracles. People are saved by the foolishness of preaching and not by the power of miracles.

For after that in the wisdom of God the world by wisdom knew not God, it pleased God by the foolishness of preaching to save them that believe.

1 Corinthians 1:21

3. God does not heal everyone because some people even hate you after they see miracles.

If I had not done among them the works which none other man did, they had not had sin: but now have they both seen and hated both me and my Father.

John 15:24

4. God does not heal everyone because people require different catalysts to help them believe.

For the Jews require a sign, and the Greeks seek after wisdom:

1 Corinthians 1:22

5. God does not heal everyone because God has determined that people should be saved by preaching and not by miracles.

    For after that in the wisdom of God the world by wisdom knew not God, it pleased God by the foolishness of preaching to save them that believe.

    1 Corinthians 1:21

There are some common misconceptions that exist about the healing ministry. Without understanding these, they will linger in our minds and influence our thinking. Dear minister of God, keep on preaching; just keep on preaching! Evangelize and tell the truth because it is the method by which God has determined that people should be saved.

We may see the power of God but we must understand that God is not trying to take away our common sense. We know that He is not trying to eradicate medicine. We know that He is not trying to outdo doctors. Above all we know that He is not replacing the need for powerful preaching of the gospel.

God has His reasons for healing. Decide today to allow preaching to affect you. Decide to believe in the simplicity of the preaching of the Word.

And the rest of the men which were not killed by these plagues yet repented not of the works of their hands, that they should not worship devils, and idols of gold, and silver, and brass, and stone, and of wood: which neither can see, nor hear, nor walk: Neither repented they of their murders, nor of their sorceries, nor of their fornication, nor of their thefts.

Revelation 9:20-21

As you can see, the people in this Scripture refused to repent in spite of all that happened to them. God knows that people will not repent even when they see certain things. We need to believe the preaching of the Word when we hear it. We do not have to look for signs before we believe.

6. God does not heal everyone because many people believe in the Word of God even without seeing miracles.

Jesus saith unto him, Thomas, because thou hast seen me, thou hast believed: blessed are they that have not seen, and yet have believed.

John 20:29

Then many of the Jews which came to Mary, and had seen the things which Jesus did, believed on him. But some of them went their ways to the Pharisees, and told them what things Jesus had done.

John 11:45-46

It is true that God heals so that people will believe. But on the other hand, there are people who believe the Word of God without seeing anything.

Jesus saith unto him, Thomas, because thou hast seen me, thou hast believed: blessed are they that have not seen, and yet have believed.

John 20:29

There are many people who don't see any miracle but believe in God. But there are some people who have to see a sign before they believe. Maybe there are people who have to be on their deathbeds before they believe in God. Some people have to lose everything before they succumb to God's love.

There are people who only get saved in prison. But you don't have to wait for that. Blessed are those who have not seen any of these things but yet believe.

The reality is that not everyone who sees miracles believes in God.

7. God does not heal everyone because He is not trying to eradicate sicknesses from the world.

Some people think that God is trying to eradicate sickness from the world through preachers. God is not trying to remove the diseases of this world through anointed ministers. His anointed apostles and prophets are not agents for the eradication of all known illnesses. If that were so, then God has failed in his quest to do so. I want you to read this passage:

And all the people saw him walking and praising God: And they knew that it was he which sat for alms at the Beautiful gate of the temple: and they were filled with wonder and amazement at that which had happened unto him. And as the lame man which was healed held Peter and John, all the people ran together unto them in the porch that is called Solomon's, greatly wondering.
Acts 3:9-11

You will notice that this man had been laid at this Beautiful Gate of the temple for many years. The Bible says he had been lame from his mother's womb. His family and relatives had carried him there many times to ask for alms from those who entered the temple.

A few weeks earlier, Jesus Himself had been walking through this Beautiful Gate of the temple. He had preached in this temple many times. Why didn't Jesus heal this man Himself? Why didn't Jesus eradicate all diseases from Jerusalem? If God is trying to eradicate illnesses from the world, why did Jesus not heal this cripple when He was here? Obviously, God does not seem to have that goal.

I have watched as many people go back from miracle services still sick. There have been documentaries that are highly critical of evangelists. One of the chief criticisms is about the many people who remain unhealed at their services.

In London, there was even a demonstration by cripples against a famous healing evangelist. How come cripples would demonstrate against a man of God?

This confusion comes about because we do not understand what God is doing and what He is not trying to do. Jesus Christ

Himself explained why He healed only one man at the Pool of Bethesda.

Then answered Jesus and said unto them, Verily, verily, I say unto you, The Son can do nothing of himself, but what he seeth the Father do: for what things soever he doeth, these also doeth the Son likewise.

John 5:19-20

Do not be disappointed when God does not heal everyone. Do not be angry with God when only one out of several sick people is healed. Jesus said, "I and my Father are one, and He that has seen me has seen the Father."

...he that hath seen me hath seen the Father...

John 14:9

Jesus is not trying to heal everybody. But He is trying to save every soul. Jesus gave His life for the whole world. He invited everyone to Heaven. "For God so loved the world that he gave his only begotten son that whosoever believeth in Him should not perish but have everlasting life" (John 3:16). Everlasting life does not depend on the healing of your kidney, your liver, your blood, your skin or your eyes.

When Jesus walked on this Earth, He knew there were many reasons why people were sick. He knew there were many reasons why God healed and equally many reasons why God didn't heal. Understand God's plan. God is trying to give you everlasting life. Jesus came to give you everlasting life. He loves us very much and He does not want any of us to perish.

God is Not Against Medicine

Unfortunately, extreme faith teachings have given the impression that God is against medicine. They have left us with the impression that God would like to replace all medical personnel with pastors. They left us with a feeling that to take medicine was sinful or unspiritual.

There was a time when many people were being healed through the faith revival. At that time, many ministers would not touch medicine. It was unheard of for a truly spiritual person to use medicine.

I heard of a church in which over forty-five people died because they refused to take medicine. There were little children who needed medication, but because of their parents' belief in faith healing, they rejected all medicine for their children. Eventually, the pastor himself became ill but refused medication. By and by, he was brought to church in a wheel chair, still refusing medical help until he died.

This kind of thing throws the healing ministry into confusion. This is why many have turned away from the healing ministry. In spite of the confusion, you cannot discount the reality of God's healing power.

We Don't Understand Everything!

God is not trying to replace hospitals and doctors with pastors and evangelists. God gave the wisdom for medical science. The two streams of healing are ordained of God and are not contrary to each other. The Bible says that Jesus Christ is the power and the wisdom of God.

But unto them which are called, both Jews and Greeks, Christ the power of God, and the wisdom of God.
1 Corinthians 1: 24

Jesus comes to help you by being the power and the wisdom of God in your life. Christians become unbalanced when they just take the power of God and leave out the wisdom. You need both the power and the wisdom. Medical science can transplant hearts today and solve many problems. Many children would be dead from various diseases like malaria, convulsions, and measles if there were no medicines.

God has given us the wisdom to think and to have common sense. One time, Jesus told His disciples to go aside and rest awhile.

And he said unto them, Come ye yourselves apart into a desert place, and rest a while: for there were many coming and going, and they had no leisure so much as to eat.

Mark 6:31

Why did Jesus tell His disciples to rest? Because there are many diseases that come from not resting. It is common sense to rest when you need to. Jesus ministered to the sick but He did sensible and practical things too.

Accept that God is Mysterious

The secret things belong unto the Lord our God: but those things which are revealed belong unto us and to our children for ever, that we may do all the words of this law.

Deuteronomy 29:29

I cannot explain why divine healing takes place the way it does. The Bible says the secret things belong to the Lord but those that are revealed belong to us.

Again the Scriptures tell us that we look through a glass dimly. This means that when you look through a glass, you cannot see things clearly. It is not everything we know and we shouldn't pretend to know everything because we do not. We definitely do not understand everything because we are looking through a glass.

For now we see through a glass, darkly; but then face to face: now I know in part; but then shall I know even as also I am known.

1 Corinthians 13:12

CHAPTER 18

Six Aspects of the Healing Anointing

1. The healing anointing prolongs life.

And when Jesus was come into Peter's house, he saw his wife's mother laid, and sick of a fever. And he touched her hand, and the fever left her: and she arose, and ministered unto them.

Matthew 8:14–15

The healing anointing heals fevers, sicknesses, headaches, and pains. It also heals heart diseases and cancers. God is a healer and Jesus is a healing Jesus. I remember once I was in a certain city, ministering at a miracle service. A lady came up with breast cancer. As a doctor, I know what breast cancer is. I prayed for her. As I was praying for her, I said, "Heal me, Lord, and I will be healed, save me and I will be saved."

Doctors can do very little about breast cancer. Cancer is often a death sentence. This lady went back to the hospital because she was supposed to have an operation. She told the doctors she believed the cancer had vanished. She reported how the doctors examined her and were surprised that the cancer had disappeared.

The healing anointing prolongs your life. The devil wants to shorten your life. But God will give you long life and prolong your days. The healing anointing will extend it! You will live and not die because there is a healing anointing coming your way right now.

2. The healing anointing heals the broken-hearted.

The heart of a person speaks of the very centre and core of the human being. A broken heart is a disappointed heart. It is a shocked and bereaved heart. Many broken-hearted people become depressed. I have had many depressed people in my miracle meetings testify about how they felt the spirit of depression leaving them. Thank God for the healing anointing, which can heal the heart.

The church is a place where the healing anointing will heal every disappointed heart. Jesus is in the business of healing disappointed hearts.

Depression is a common and serious illness. Suicide is a common thing among depressed people. I have seen different people commit suicide. Medical students have committed suicide. I have seen doctors commit suicide. I have seen men with good jobs in the United Nations commit suicide. I have seen church members with apparently normal and blessed lives commit suicide. These people were probably depressed and felt life was hopeless.

God can heal depression through His power. In the medical world, drugs and electric shocks are used to treat depression. Thank God for the healing anointing, which heals the broken-hearted and depressed people of this world.

3. The healing anointing heals the "will" of men.

The healing anointing heals the soul, which consists of the intellect, the will and the emotions of man. The inability of some people to say "no" to things that destroy them is a sign of a diseased will. Some people cannot say "no" to drinking, smoking and sex. The healing anointing heals you of the inability to take decisions.

4. The healing anointing heals the souls of men.

He restoreth my soul:

Psalm 23:3

The soul is devastated by sin. Our emotions and minds are often damaged by experiences we have had. Through the healing anointing, we receive restoration to our minds, our wills and our emotions. Some people cannot love anyone! Others cannot receive love! These are all symptoms of damaged and wounded people who need healing.

I once watched a documentary of a nineteen-year-old black American who was a serial bank robber. He escaped from jail many times until he was put in a maximum security prison for life. I watched with compassion as this teenager with a diseased mind was caged like an animal for life. Why do you think so many American men are in jail? They are wounded and diseased in their souls. These are people broken by years of discrimination, poverty, racism and fatherlessness.

5. The healing anointing heals men who are demon-possessed.

And he came down with them, and stood in the plain, and the company of the disciples, and a great multitude of people out of all Judaea and Jerusalem, and from the coast of Tyre and Sidon, which came near to hear him, and to be healed of their diseases; AND THEY THAT WERE VEXED WITH UNCLEAN SPIRITS: AND THEY WERE HEALED.

Luke 6:17, 18

People who were set free from evil spirits were said to be healed. The healing anointing touches lives afflicted by demons. The healing anointing is not just for the healing of sicknesses but for healing the effects of demon oppression. When the healing anointing is present, it drives away evil spirits.

162

How God anointed Jesus of Nazareth with the Holy Ghost and with power: who went about doing good, and HEALING ALL THAT WERE OPPRESSED OF THE DEVIL; for God was with him.

Acts 10:38

Many people have evil spirits. Anybody who is oppressed by the devil or has any demonic activity in his life needs the healing anointing. Jesus healed people who were vexed with unclean spirits.

Demons see people as homes they can live in. Many people who are delivered from evil spirits testify that they feel something going out of them. The human being is like a house with many rooms.

Jesus described how evil spirits see human beings as houses where they can live. A house has many rooms. Some of the rooms of the house are used more than others. The rooms of a human being could be his mind, his temperament, his flesh, his heart, his attitude, his emotion, his will and his understanding.

When the unclean spirit is gone out of a man, he walketh through dry places, seeking rest, and findeth none.

Then he saith, I will return into my house from whence I came out; and when he is come, he findeth it empty, swept, and garnished.

Then goeth he, and taketh with himself seven other spirits more wicked than himself, and they enter in and dwell there...

Matthew 12:43-45

There are people whose emotions and moods are occupied by evil spirits. Some people become moody so often that it is clear that their moods are occupied by demons. No one is able to stay around such people when they get into their moods.

Some people have evil spirits occupying their sexual lives. Unbridled sexuality is usually caused by the presence of evil

163

spirits. Others have evil spirits in their minds and understanding. Stubbornness and the lack of understanding could well be a sign of the presence of demons. Through the power of the Holy Spirit, healing comes to all these afflicted areas.

6. The healing anointing breaks the yoke.

And it shall come to pass in that day, that his burden shall be taken away from off thy shoulder, and his yoke from off thy neck, and the yoke shall be destroyed because of the anointing.

Isaiah 10:27

A yoke is something that keeps you captive in such a way that you can't come out. A yoke is something you can't stop or get away from. Blindness and paralysis are yokes.

A yoke is a heavy burden that keeps you fixed in a particular state so that your movement and freedom are limited. A cow, which is under a yoke, is fixed in a particular state. It cannot move to the left or to the right. It's under a yoke. A yoke is a fixation. The anointing of the Holy Spirit is a yoke-breaking and a yoke-destroying anointing. It will heal anything that has tied and fixed you. The healing anointing can break the yokes in people's lives. Some people seem doomed to die tragically no matter what they do. That is the yoke of death. There are some people who are told by the devil that they will divorce when they marry. Divorce seems to be their destiny. They seem to be destined and tied to unhappiness in marriage.

Some nations are under yokes. No matter what they do and what type of governments they have, they go in a particular direction.

A yoke is something that is tied around your neck that pulls you in a particular direction. You will realize that almost everything about our lives requires healing. When the healing anointing begins to flow, the burdens will be taken off the shoulders of the people. The yokes will be removed from people through the healing anointing.

Through the anointing, the yokes will be broken and you will have the opportunity to preach to thousands.

It Is Time to Gather Whole Cities!

And at even, when the sun did set, they brought unto him all that were diseased, and them that were possessed with devils. And all the city was gathered together at the door. And he healed many that were sick of divers diseases, and cast out many devils; and suffered not the devils to speak, because they knew him.

Mark 1:32-34

The healing anointing is your opportunity to gather the whole city to your church. The healing anointing is our opportunity to gather the whole city to our crusades. The work of God will enter a new dimension when we operate in the healing anointing of Christ.

CHAPTER 19

Seven Characteristics of the Healing Anointing

1. **The healing anointing is the anointing upon you and not the anointing within you.**

   But the anointing which ye have received of him abideth in you, and ye need not that any man teach you: but as the same anointing teacheth you of all things, and is truth, and is no lie, and even as it hath taught you, ye shall abide in him.

   1 John 2:27

   The anointing upon you is different from the anointing in you. Many people do not understand the difference. We can all be filled with the Holy Spirit and rivers of living water will flow out of our bellies.

   He that believeth on me, as the scripture hath said, out of his belly shall flow rivers of living water.

   John 7:38

   Since we all have these rivers of living waters flowing out of us, don't we all have the healing anointing? The anointing every Christian has is the anointing within. Jesus also claimed to have something within Him. He claimed to have God in Him. And yet He knew when the mantle of the healing anointing had come upon Him.

But if I do, though ye believe not me, believe the works: that ye may know, and believe, that the Father is in me, and I in him.

John 10:38

The healing anointing is another anointing that God places upon the minister. That is why Jesus said, "The Spirit of the Lord is upon me...."

The Spirit of the Lord is upon me, because he hath anointed me to preach the gospel to the poor; he hath sent me to heal the brokenhearted, to preach deliverance to the captives, and recovering of sight to the blind, to set at liberty them that are bruised,

Luke 4:18

It is like a cloak that comes upon the minister. When the Lord told me that He was giving me a healing anointing, He was not filling me with a new anointing. I was already filled with the Spirit. He was putting an anointing upon me. That is why the anointing is sometimes referred to as a cloak or a mantle. A mantle is something you put on. It is not something that you swallow or you take in. It typifies the anointing that comes upon a person for special ministry.

2. The healing anointing is activated by faith.

The anointing is activated by faith. The anointing will not work when there is a lot of doubt. The woman with the issue of blood had faith in the power of God. She didn't know Him personally. She had just heard that there was power around Him. She felt that the power could even be in His clothes. She touched the hem of His garment and virtue flowed out of Jesus and into her body.

For she said, If I may touch but his clothes, I shall be whole. And he said unto her, Daughter, thy faith hath

167

made thee whole; go in peace, and be whole of thy plague.

Mark 5:28, 34

Jesus was on His way to someone's house when He felt the pull on His clothes. Suddenly, He knew that virtue had gone out of Him. Jesus turned round in the crowd and asked who had touched Him.

The disciples were not happy when they found out who it was. It is often like that. The disciples who should have been in the flow were walking around and probably yawning, and getting tired of all the people. They just wanted to enjoy their privileges as Jesus' bodyguards. The lady told Jesus all that had happened. She was uneasy because she felt people might think that she was trying to undress Jesus in public. But she had felt the power of God going through her.

The only thing Jesus said to her was, "Daughter, thy faith had made thee whole."

In this statement, Jesus revealed the key to the flow of the anointing. Faith is the key that draws out the anointing from the anointed one. I have noticed that people who have faith in me draw out the gift of God in me. The faith they have in me actually draws out the gift in me and makes a demand on the anointing. You must really believe in a person to touch the hem of his garment for your healing. Absolute trust in a person causes the anointing to be stirred up. It is real.

One day, Elisha was passing through a town. A woman asked her husband to make a room for the man of God. Once again, we see a woman recognizing the anointing before the man notices anything at all.

She told her husband, "Let's do something for this man of God who is passing through the town." The husband agreed and she prepared a nice place for the prophet to live.

One day, Elisha asked the lady, "What do you want from God?" That is the question that the anointing asks everyone who

168

walks by faith. What do you want? When you have faith, the anointing is stirred up and begins to ask—what do you want? What do you need? What is your desire?"

> And it fell on a day, that Elisha passed to Shunem where was a great woman, and she constrained him to eat bread. And so it was, that as oft as he passed by, he turned in thither to eat bread. And she said unto her husband, Behold now, I perceive that this is an holy man of God, which passeth by us continually.
>
> Let us make a little chamber, I pray thee, on the wall; and let us set for him there a bed and a table, and a stool and a candlestick: and it shall be, when he cometh to us, that he shall turn to thither.
>
> And it fell on a day, that he came thither, and he turned into the chamber, and lay there.
>
> 2 Kings 4:8-11

The woman said, "I live in my own hometown and with my own people." She needed a child. God gave it to her because she had stirred up the anointing on Elisha!

Your faith is what will make you whole. Have faith in God. Have faith in God's servants. Have faith in the healing anointing.

3. The healing anointing is quenched by familiarity.

Jesus went to His own hometown to preach. He was a known carpenter from Nazareth. They couldn't believe that the same carpenter was saying He had been anointed to preach, heal and set captives free. "How absurd," they must have thought to themselves.

> And he went out from thence, and came into his own country; and his disciples follow him. And when the Sabbath day was come, he began to teach in the synagogue: many hearing him were astonished, saying, From whence hath this man these things?

And what wisdom is this which is given unto him, that even such mighty works are wrought by his hands?

Is not this the carpenter, the son of Mary, the brother of James, and Joses and of Juda, and Simon? and are not his sisters here with us?

And they were offended at him.

But Jesus said unto them, A prophet is not without honour, but in his own country, and among his own kin, and in his own house. And he could there do no mighty work, save that he laid his hands upon a few sick folk, and healed them.

Mark 6:1-5

Jesus had repaired their beds, cupboards and wardrobes for many years. They knew Him as a carpenter and not as a deliverer. The anointing is quenched by familiarity. Familiarity breeds contempt!

Sometimes, it is better for you to stay at a good distance so you can receive anointing. Sometimes when you are close to a man of God, you tend to despise him. It takes grace to be close and still be able to receive. Not everybody has that grace!

See Good? See Bad? See Anointing?

Familiarity breeds questions, which kill the anointing. But this daughter with the issue of blood believed that if she could touch the hem of Jesus' garment, she would be made whole. She didn't know whether He was a carpenter or a plumber. And it didn't matter to her. It is a good thing if Jesus was a carpenter but that is not the point when it comes to the power of God.

You must set aside analytical or critical thoughts and think in terms of the power of God. The woman didn't care who His father or mother were. She didn't know how much Jesus had charged to make one king-sized bed. It was the last thing on her mind. She could not see good, she could not see bad, she could only see the power of God. And that is what she got! She received the power.

Decrease the Familiarity, Increase the Anointing

This is why men of God seem to be more anointed when they are out of their own churches. The further they are from the familiar people, the more the anointing flows.

It is not because they are more anointed when they travel. It is because there is less familiarity when a minister travels away from his home. Jesus Christ Himself could not do much when He came to His own country.

4. The healing anointing has been proven to be real by medical science.

Medical science is not at variance with the healing anointing. Jesus asked the man to go to the place where people are officially declared healed. That is today's equivalent of a hospital.

> And there came a leper to him, beseeching him, and kneeling down to him, and saying unto him, If thou wilt, thou canst make me clean.
>
> And Jesus, moved with compassion, put forth his hand, and touched him, and saith unto him, I will; be thou clean. And as soon as he had spoken immediately the leprosy departed from him, and he was cleansed.
>
> And he straitly charged him, and forthwith sent him away; And saith unto him, See thou say nothing to any man: but go thy way, shew thyself to the priest, and offer for thy cleansing those things which Moses commanded, for a testimony unto them.
>
> Mark 1:40-44

Healing can stand the tests of medical science. Jesus knew that His power could stand the test of science. If God has healed you and you are truly healed, your healing can stand the test of any medical examination. I want you to know that God's healing is as real as any other healing.

I remember the miracle healing of a diabetic lady who lived on daily insulin injections. She had fasted and believed that God would heal her. She kept checking her blood sugar levels all the time during the meeting to see if she was healed. After the miracle service, she went back to see her doctors. The doctors did a couple of tests and found no evidence of diabetes. They apologized to her for mistakenly diagnosing her as a diabetic.

Scientific Evidence of Prayer and Healing

Science is now documenting the fact that faith in God is able to heal the sick. I would like to quote a very interesting article from the October, 1999 issue of Reader's Digest:

The notion that religious faith can promote physical well-being is not new. Most of us have heard of cases in which someone, seemingly by sheer faith and will, has miraculously recovered from a terminal illness or survived far longer than doctors thought possible. What is new is that such rewards of religion are becoming the stuff of science.

"We cannot prove scientifically that God heals, but I believe we can prove that belief in God has a beneficial effect," declares Dale A. Matthew, M.D., associate professor of medicine at Georgetown University Medical Center in Washington, D.C. "There's little doubt that healthy religious faith and practices can help people get better."

Compelling Evidence

Just how powerful is the evidence linking faith and health? More than 30 studies have found a connection between spiritual or religious commitment and longer life. Among the most compelling:
A survey of 5,286 Californians found that church members have lower death rates than non-members, regardless of risk factors such as smoking, drinking, obesity, and inactivity.

Those with a religious commitment had fewer symptoms or had better health outcomes in seven out of eight cancer studies, four out of five blood pressure studies, four out of six heart disease studies, and four out of five general health studies.

People with a strong religious commitment seem to be less prone to depression, suicide, alcoholism, and other addictions, according to one research analysis.

One of the most extensive reviews demonstrates that the connections between religion and health cut across age, sex, cultural, and geographic boundaries. It includes more than 200 studies in which religion was found to be a factor in the incidence of a disease, explains Jeffrey S. Levin, a former professor at Eastern Virginia Medical School in Norfolk. Levin found an association between good health and religion in studies of children and older adults; of U.S. Protestants, European Catholics, Japanese Buddhists, and Israeli Jews; of people living in the 1930's and 1980's; of patients suffering from acute and chronic diseases.

How Prayer Heals

Why does faith appear to have such a powerful protective effect? Experts offer several possible explanations.

Going to religious services guarantees contact with people. Social support is a well-documented key to health and longevity.

Faith gives a sense of hope and control that counteracts stress. "Commitment to a system of beliefs enables people to better handle traumatic illness, suffering, and loss," says Harold G. Koenig, M.D., director of the center for the study of religion, spirituality, and health at Duke University Medical Center.

Praying evokes beneficial changes in the body. When people pray, they experience the same decreases in blood pressure, metabolism, heart and breathing rates as the famous "relaxation response" described by Herbert Benson, M.D. of the Harvard Medical School. Reciting the rosary, for example, involves the same steps as the relaxation response: repeating a word, prayer, phrase, or sound, and returning to the repetition when other thoughts intrude. While the relaxation response works regardless of the words used, Benson says, those who choose a religious phrase are more likely to benefit if they believe in God.

Can Others' Prayers Heal?

Researchers are investigating whether the prayers of others can heal. Benson and his colleagues, studying coronary-bypass patients, and Matthews, studying people with rheumatoid arthritis, are trying to confirm findings of an oft-quoted 1988 study by cardiologist Randolph Byrd, M.D.

Dr. Byrd divided 393 heart patients in San Francisco General Hospital Medical Center into two groups. One was prayed for by Christians around the country; the other did not receive prayers from study participants. Patients did not know to which group they belonged. The group that was prayed for experienced fewer complications, fewer cases of pneumonia, fewer cardiac arrests, less congestive heart failure, and needed fewer antibiotics.

Even more confounding are controversial studies suggesting prayer can influence everything from the growth of bacteria in a lab to healing wounds in mice. "These studies on lower organisms can be done with great scientific precision, and the findings can't be explained away by, say, the placebo effect," says Larry Dossey, M.D., author of Prayer Is Good Medicine.

Doctors as Believers

Dr. Dossey became so convinced of the power of prayer that he began to pray privately for his patients. Nevertheless, he and other experts tread cautiously in this area. "We certainly don't want to start selling religion in the name of science," he says. "People need to make their own choices."

And yet, health care institutions are beginning to pay attention to the faith-health connection. Conferences on spirituality and health have been sponsored by Harvard Medical School and the Mayo Clinic. Nearly half of U.S. medical schools now offer courses on the topic. In a survey of 269 doctors at the 1996 meeting of the American Academy of Family Physicians, 99% said they thought religious beliefs could contribute to healing. When asked about their personal experiences, 63% of doctors said God intervened to improve their own medical conditions.

Clearly, their patients agree that prayer is a powerful tool in healing. Polls by Time/CNN and USA Weekend show that about 80% of Americans believe spiritual faith or prayer can help people recover from illness or injury, and more than 60% think doctors should talk to patients about faith and even pray with those who request it.

This yearning for a connection between religion and medicine is partly a reaction to a health care system that has become increasingly rushed and impersonal. "In medicine, the pendulum had swung so far toward the physical that it almost totally excluded anything spiritual," Dr. Dossey says. "This didn't feel right to patients or many physicians, and the pendulum has begun to swing back."

How Faith Fits In

So what does this mean for the average person? It does not mean adding worship to the list of healthy things you can do. You can't adopt faith as you would a low-fat diet.

What you can do is speak up if you're facing illness or surgery and would like your belief to be part of your health care. That doesn't mean you should expect your doctor to pray with or for you. But it's reasonable to expect him to listen to your needs, arrange a visit from the hospital chaplain, or allow time for prayer before you're wheeled into the operating room.

"Faith" Koenig maintains, "Offers people some control over their lives as opposed to just depending on a medical profession that's becoming more distant and mechanized every day.

The healing anointing is real!

5. The healing anointing is a lingering anointing.

There was a man who was raised from the dead when he came into contact with Elisha's bones. Apparently there was a lingering anointing in the grave. Elisha's grave still contained some anointing. Allow the anointing to linger on you. Don't be in a hurry to move out of the anointing. Anyone who has had hands laid upon him in a miracle service has a lingering anointing resting upon him. The anointing stays around for a long time. It is a lingering anointing.

> And Elisha died, and they buried him. And the bands of the Moabites invaded the land at the coming in of the year. And it came to pass, as they were burying a man, that, behold they spied a band of men; and they cast the man into the sepulchre of Elisha: and when the man was let down and touched the bones of Elisha, he revived, and stood up on his feet.
>
> 2 Kings 13: 20-21

6. The healing anointing is mysterious.

Now Elisha was fallen sick of his sickness whereof he died.

2 Kings 13:14

Someone may ask, "Why did Elisha's anointing not heal Elisha himself?" Why was the anointing which could raise the dead not able to heal the vessel which was carrying the anointing? The healing anointing is a mysterious anointing. Many wonder why one person is healed and another is not. How is it that someone who has died of sickness, can still minister healing?

7. The healing anointing is associated with the anointing for prosperity.

The healing anointing is associated with prosperity. Healing is usually accompanied by prosperity.

Throughout the Bible you will notice the association between healing and prosperity. You will notice that people who preach about healing often preach about prosperity.

a. Isaiah the prophet linked healing and prosperity.

The Spirit of the Lord GOD is upon me; because the LORD hath anointed me to preach good tidings unto the meek; he hath sent me to bind up the brokenhearted, to proclaim liberty to the captives, and the opening of the prison to them that are bound;
To proclaim the acceptable year of the LORD, and the day of vengeance of our God; to comfort all that mourn;

To appoint unto them that mourn in Zion, to give unto them beauty for ashes, the oil of joy for mourning, the garment of praise for the spirit of heaviness; that they might be called trees of righteousness, the planting of the LORD, that he might be glorified.

Isaiah 61:1-3

Somebody may wonder why they always teach about these two things. It is because they go together. Jesus spoke of the anointing, "The Spirit of the Lord is upon me," He declared that He had been anointed to preach the gospel to the POOR.

First of all, He addressed the needs of the poor. Then in the very next sentence he spoke of healing the broken-hearted.

The introduction of Jesus' ministry, prosperity and healing are linked together. When the healing anointing is flowing, prosperity abounds. When people receive healing these two miracles move together.

Why did God heal you and extend your life? To bless you with more years of abundance over here.

b. John the apostle linked healing and prosperity.

Beloved, I wish above all things that you thou mayest prosper and be in health, even as thy soul prospereth.

3 John 2

John the apostle also linked these two blessings. He declared that his greatest wish was for his spiritual children to have both prosperity and healing.

Once again, the two blessings are together. If God has given you healing, He's given you prosperity as well. It's real!

There is healing on the left and prosperity on the right. Prosperity and healing walk together. When you receive one, open your eyes because the other one is nearby.

c. Jesus Christ linked healing and prosperity.

And he said unto them, ye will surely say unto me this proverb, Physician, heal thyself: whatsoever we have heard done in Capernaum, do also here in thy country.

But I tell you of a truth, many widows were in Israel in the days of Elias, when the heaven was shut up three years and six months, when great famine was throughout all the land; But unto none of them was Elias sent, save unto Sarepta, a city of Sidon, unto a woman that was a widow.

And many lepers were in Israel in the time of Eliseus the prophet; and none of them was cleansed, saving Naaman the Syrian.

Luke 4:23, 24-27

Jesus linked healing and prosperity when He taught about the healing of Naaman and the prosperity of the widow in one sermon.

In Jesus' famous hometown sermon, He spoke about both healing and prosperity. He spoke of the healing of Naaman the Syrian. In the same breath, he spoke of the financial miracle of the widow of Zarephath. These two blessings seem to be linked in the spirit. I see the Lord giving you the prosperity and the healing that you need.

CHAPTER 20

Four Ways You Can Receive the Healing Anointing

...who can heal thee?

Lamentations 2:13

The question is clear, "Who can heal thee?" Many of the diseases in this world cannot really be cured by medical science. Usually, doctors control the effects of diseases. Many things are done just to keep a patient alive. God is a healer and that is why He introduced Himself in the Old Testament as Jehovah Rophe. He is Jehovah your healer, the bridge builder, the healer of your life, the healer of your situations, and the giver of hope.

People often don't understand other people's problems. Many times we try to sympathize with the victims but we don't really understand the extent of the problem they face. Sickness and disease is one of the greatest problems of mankind. Who can heal thee? The Lord can heal thee!

1. **You can receive the healing anointing through the laying on of hands.**

   ...they shall lay hands on the sick, and they shall recover.

   Mark 16:18

One of the ways that God can touch you and bless you is through the laying on of hands. Don't take the laying on of hands for granted. Something wonderful happens when hands are laid on you by an anointed person.

There was a time that Dr. Yonggi Cho was laying hands on people in the Prayer Mountain. Soon there was a queue of people who wanted to receive a touch. I said to myself, "Well, once I can see a hand being stretched out, I shall not leave this place without that hand being laid on me." I joined the queue immediately and received my part of the blessing. As soon as hands were laid on me I said to myself, "Thank you Lord, something is happening to me right now."

I know that the anointing is passed on when hands are laid on you and so I believe that even shaking hands with the man of God can transmit the anointing.

I remember a story I heard about Archbishop Benson Idahosa when he was returning to Nigeria from Bible School. He was just about to start out in ministry and his church officials had come to the airport to meet him. As he shook hands with them, they began to fall under the power. It is faith in the contact that activates the anointing.

The laying on of hands is based on the principle that the power of God is transmitted through physical contact. Even a hug, a handshake or mere physical contact can lead to the transmission of the anointing. A simple hug can become as powerful as laying on of hands depending on what you are believing God for! When a dead body fell into Elisha's grave, he came back to life because the power of God was transmitted to him by the power of contact.

2. You can receive the healing anointing through the anointing oil.

And they cast out many devils, AND ANOINTED WITH OIL MANY THAT WERE SICK, AND HEALED THEM.

Mark 6:13

Is any sick among you? let him call for the elders of the church; and let them pray over him, ANOINTING HIM WITH OIL IN THE NAME OF THE LORD: And the prayer of faith shall save the sick, and the Lord shall raise him up; and if he hath committed sins, they shall be forgiven him.

James 5:14-15

Praying for the sick with anointing oil is scriptural. Our simple olive oil is like the Balm of Gilead and it represents the anointing of Almighty God. If you can believe that it is no more ordinary olive oil, but the healing anointing of the Holy Spirit, it will heal every disease in your life. It is the anointing oil that healed the sick and cast out devils in the Bible. It is real!

Remember what Jesus said about the communion. He said it was His body and His blood. He told us to eat His body and drink His blood.

And as they were eating, Jesus took bread, and blessed it, and brake it, and gave it to the disciples, and said, Take, eat; THIS IS MY BODY.

And he took the cup, and gave thanks, and gave it to them, saying, Drink ye all of it; For THIS IS MY BLOOD of the new testament, which is shed for many for the remission of sins.

Matthew 26:26-28

When some people took the communion and believed that it was no longer bread or just wine but actually the body and blood of Jesus, they were healed. When others treated it disrespectfully they became sick and some died.

Wherefore whosoever shall eat this bread, and drink this cup of the Lord, unworthily, shall be guilty of the body and blood of the Lord. But let a man examine himself, and so let him eat of that bread, and drink of that cup.

For he that eateth and drinketh unworthily, eateth and drinketh damnation to himself, not discerning the Lord's body. For this cause many are weak and sickly among you, and many sleep.

1 Corinthians 11:27-30

In the same way, you must understand that when we pray over the oil that it is no longer oil but the power of the Holy Spirit passing into your body.

3. You can receive the healing anointing through garments.

Many people do not recognize the power of the anointing that resides within the clothes of anointed people. The healing anointing seems to be able to stay in the garments of anointed people. The woman with the issue of blood believed that she did not need to be prayed for or be anointed with oil. She didn't need to meet or speak to Jesus personally. If only she could touch His garment, she would be healed.

For she said, IF I MAY TOUCH BUT HIS CLOTHES, I shall be whole.

Mark 5:28

The invisible power of the Holy Spirit is translated into the physical. That is why physical methods like the laying on of hands, the anointing with oil and the coming into contact with garments can transmit the power of the Holy Spirit. Notice how a whole city just wanted to touch the garments of Jesus. They were not interested in prayer, counselling or anything like that. They just wanted to touch His clothes.

And when they were gone over, they came into the land of Gennesaret. And when the men of that place had knowledge of him, they sent out into all that country round about, and brought unto him all that were diseased; And besought him THAT THEY MIGHT ONLY TOUCH THE HEM OF HIS GARMENT: AND AS MANY AS TOUCHED WERE MADE PERFECTLY WHOLE.

Matthew 14:34-36

When people have faith, the anointing is activated. The men of the city just wanted to touch the hem of whatever Jesus was wearing. They knew that the anointing was in the garment.

One day, two prophets were walking by the river, one was anointed and the other was not. The one who was not anointed wanted desperately to catch the anointing. As they walked along, the younger prophet asked the older prophet if he could have twice as much of his anointing. The older prophet laughed and said that he had asked a hard thing.

Suddenly, a chariot of fire appeared and even though the younger prophet tried to stay close, the older prophet was whisked away to heaven. The younger prophet was so sad that he cried. When he had finished crying, he wiped his tears and looked around him. AND THERE WAS THE GARMENT! It had been left behind. The young prophet knew that the anointing could be in the garment. He took up the garment (mantle) and smote the waters of the river Jordan. "Where is the Lord God of Elijah?" he cried. He wasn't sure whether it was an anointed garment or not.

But when the river responded to the mantle, the young prophet knew that he had picked up an anointed garment. The garment contained the anointing and he had the garment. His life was going to be different because he had the anointing.

> And it came to pass, when they were gone over, that Elijah said unto Elisha, Ask what I shall do for thee. before I be taken away from thee.
>
> And Elisha said, I pray thee, let a double portion of thy spirit be upon me. And he said, Thou hast asked a hard thing: nevertheless, if thou see me when I am taken from thee, it shall be so unto thee; but if not, it shall not be so.
>
> And it came to pass, as they still went on, and talked, that, behold, there appeared a chariot of fire, and horses of fire, and parted them both asunder; and Elijah went up by a whirlwind into heaven.
>
> And Elisha saw it, and he cried, My father, my father, the chariot of Israel, and the horsemen thereof. And he saw him no more: and he took hold of his own clothes, and rent them in two pieces.
>
> He took up also the mantle of Elijah that fell from him, and went back, and stood by the bank of Jordan; and he took the mantle of Elijah that fell from him, and smote the waters, and said, where is the LORD GOD of Elijah? and when he also had smitten the waters, they parted hither and thither: and Elisha went over.
>
> 2 Kings 2:9-14

You can't define God and put Him in a box. You can't expect God to behave in a particular way. The healing anointing is mysterious! All these different ways are biblical methods that make the anointing flow.

4. **You can receive the healing anointing through the spoken word.**

The healing anointing works by the spoken word. It is called the "rhema". Jesus hardly laid hands on people. He mostly ministered by speaking words to them.

He would say, "Go thy way, thy son liveth" or He would say, "Daughter, thy faith has made thee whole."

On another occasion, he said, "Young man, I say unto thee, arise."

Most people want hands to be laid on them but many miracles take place through the spoken word.

Elisha and the Spoken Word

Elisha operated in the healing anointing by speaking a word. Elisha sent a message to Naaman: "Go and wash and thou shalt be made whole." The healing was in that message.

So Naaman came with his horses and with his chariot, and stood at the door of the house of Elisha. And Elisha sent a messenger unto him, saying, Go and wash in Jordan seven times, and thy flesh shall come again to thee, and thou shalt be clean.

2 Kings 5:9-10

Jesus and the Spoken Word

There was a nobleman's son who was not well. The man came to Jesus for the healing of his son. Jesus said to him, "Go thy way, thy son liveth." No prayer. No laying on of hands. No anointing oil. No garment. Just a word! Speaking a word is a powerful way of ministering healing.

On his way home, this nobleman met some people who told him that his son was healed. He inquired of them what time the son had improved and found out that it was at the same time that Jesus had spoken to him. Only six words had been spoken. A great miracle had taken place.

> **So Jesus came again into Cana...there was a certain nobleman, whose son was sick at Capernaum. When he heard that Jesus was come out of Judea into Galilee, he went unto him and besought him that he would come down, and heal his son: for he was at the point of death...**
>
> **Jesus saith unto him, Go thy way, thy son liveth.... And as he was now going down his servants met him, and told him, saying, Thy son liveth.**
>
> **Then enquired he of them the hour when he began to amend.**
>
> **And they said unto him, Yesterday at the seventh hour the fever left him. So the father knew that it was at the same hour, in the which Jesus said unto him, Thy son liveth...**
>
> **John 4:46, 47, 50-53**

Try not to think so much about hands being laid on you. God will touch you and change your life through the spoken word of His anointed servant.

CHAPTER 21

Operate in the Power and Fire of the Spirit

1. **Be honest and accept the fact that you lack the power dimension of the Holy Spirit.**

Believe that you must operate in the power dimension of the anointing. Do whatever you need to do to lift yourself from an ordinary anointing into a power anointing.

The Scriptures show a clear difference between the ordinary anointing and the power dimension of the anointing. Jesus went away being led by the anointing but returned under the power of the anointing. Jesus Christ was anointed with the Holy Spirit and with power.

How God anointed Jesus of Nazareth with the HOLY GHOST AND WITH POWER: who went about doing good, and healing all that were oppressed of the devil; for God was with him.
Acts 10:38

Many of us know the fruit of the Holy Spirit, such as love, patience, peace and joy. We believe that these qualities are what the Holy Spirit brings to our lives. Indeed, the love, joy, peace, patience, longsuffering and gentleness of the Holy Spirit are precious fruits.

We also know that He baptizes us and helps us to speak in tongues. But there is more. There is also the power dimension. There is a difference between the anointing of the Holy Spirit and the power of the Holy Spirit. These two are mentioned separately for a reason.

The Bible separates the *anointing* and the *power* for you to understand that they are different. Why did the Bible not just say that Jesus had been anointed with the Holy Spirit? Because there is a difference between having the Holy Spirit and having the *power* of the Holy Spirit.

God is showing us that there is a power dimension to the Holy Spirit. Thank God you are anointed. But God is trying to give you both the anointing *and* the power.

And Jesus being full of the Holy Spirit returned from Jordan, and WAS LED BY THE SPIRIT into the wilderness,

Luke 4:1

2. **Allow yourself to be led by the Holy Spirit into the power dimension.**

And Jesus returned in THE POWER OF THE SPIRIT into Galilee: and there went out a fame of him through all the region round about.

Luke 4:14

You must be able to follow the Holy Spirit even if He leads you to the wilderness. This is how you will encounter the power dimension. I entered into the power dimension of the Holy Spirit by being led by God into it.

Jesus was "led by the Spirit" to go into the wilderness. When He came back, He operated in the "power of the Spirit". Every pastor can be anointed with the Holy Spirit. But every pastor can also be anointed with power. Your ministry will change when you have both the Holy Spirit and the power of the Holy Spirit. You can be a beautiful teacher of the Word of God but you can also have a power dimension to your teaching ministry.

3. Believe in the fire dimension of the Holy Ghost.

Notice what John the Baptist said about Jesus. He said Jesus would have both the Holy Spirit and fire.

John answered, saying unto them all, I indeed baptize you with water; but one mightier than I cometh, the latchet of whose shoes I am not worthy to unloose: he shall baptize you with the HOLY GHOST AND WITH FIRE:

Luke 3:16

Once again, you will notice that fire is mentioned separately. There is a fire dimension of the Holy Spirit. Fire is a type of power. Jesus did not just have the anointing; He had the power and the fire of the anointing.

There is a fire dimension of ministry. The fire of the Holy Spirit will burn every chaff and every wicked work of the devil. That is the dimension of the anointing that God is trying to bring us into. It is the tangible dimension. It is the power and the fire.

May you constantly operate in the power and the fire dimension of the Holy Spirit. [77]May you enjoy ministering with miracles and manifestations of the Holy Spirit!